ID006506

Meditations for Moms

Hope and Laughter for Mothers of All Ages

Meditations for Moms

Hope
and
Laughter
for Mothers
of All
Ages

Crystal Bowman

Baker Books

A Division of Baker Book House Co
Grand Rapids, Michigan 49516

Published by Baker Books
a division of Baker Book House Company
P.O. Box 6287, Grand Rapids, MI 49516-6287

Printed in the United States of America

Library of Congress Cataloging-in-Publication Data

Bowman, Crystal.
    Meditations for moms : hope and laughter for mothers of all ages / Crystal Bowman.
        p.   cm.
    ISBN: 0-8010-1224-4 (hardcover)
    1. Mothers—Religious life. 2. Motherhood—Religious aspects—Christianity—Meditations. I. Title.
BV4847.B595   2001
242'.6431—dc21   2001025759

The names of some persons mentioned in this book have been changed in order to protect their privacy.

For current information about all releases from Baker Book House, visit our web site:

http://www.bakerbooks.com

To Helen Stewart, Ruthie Krause, and Nancy Samra
for their inspiration to women and their faithfulness to God.

Special thanks to:
Helen Postma
Susie Broadhead
Teri Bowman

Contents

Introduction

The meditations in this book are from one mother to another. They were inspired by children, friends, and grandmothers and have been composed over the years during tennis meets, gymnastic lessons, and hockey practices. The rough drafts were scribbled on paper napkins, spelling tests, and grocery receipts. They are real stories about real people, personal prayers from my heart, and poems from the depths of my soul.

Some of the meditations will put a smile on your face, while others may bring a tear to your eye. They were created to offer hope and encouragement, comfort and laughter.

As you read, reflect, and meditate, you may see yourself between the lines. But above all, may you be reminded of the love and faithfulness of God.

 Crystal

The Fan

"Obey the LORD your God and follow his commands and decrees that I give you today."

Deuteronomy 27:10

I enjoyed the convenience and comfort of having my grandmother live next door to me when I was growing up. If Mom wasn't home, Grandma was. If Mom didn't have something, Grandma did. My siblings and I had the privilege of going in and out of her home as though it was our own, and we always helped ourselves to the pink and white peppermints she kept in the milk glass candy dish on her bedroom dresser.

Every Sunday, Grandma attended church with us and came to our house for dinner. She often contributed something fresh, homemade, and delicious to our meal. One summer Sunday, as we sat down to eat, my mother noticed that we were almost out of butter. When Grandma offered to donate a stick from her refrigerator, I volunteered to get it. As I went out the back door to walk across our driveway to Grandma's house, she hollered out to me, "Don't stick your finger in the fan!"

Since those were the days before air-conditioning, Grandma had a small portable fan on her kitchen table. As I passed by the table on my way to the refrigerator, I took one look at the fan and promptly stuck my finger into the large spinning blades. Fortunately, the blades were rather dull and rotating at slow speed. I only sustained a minor cut on my finger, but the oozing blood required a bandage, which I found in Grandma's medicine cabinet. After bandaging my injured finger, I finally opened the refrigerator door and removed the stick of butter—which was, after all, the purpose for the trip.

As I walked back into our house and placed the butter in the empty butter dish, everyone immediately noticed my bandaged finger. Through tears, I confessed my act of disobedience to a stunned audience.

So why did I stick my finger in the fan? Because Grandma told me not to do it. If she had said to me, "Stick your finger in the fan when you walk by the table," I never would have done it! There is something about our human nature that makes us desire what we can't have or do what we're told not to do.

In the Book of Genesis, God tells Adam and Eve that they may eat from all of the trees in the garden except one. Seems like a fair deal to me. But what does Eve do? She takes a bite of the forbidden fruit and changes her life and the course of history forever.

The Ten Commandments found in Exodus 20 are not the "ten suggestions." They are laws designed by God to protect us from harm and to help us live safe, happy lives.

Obedience to God's laws will result in his blessings, whereas disobedience can result in emotional or physical consequences. The more we read and study God's Word, the more we will understand that God's laws are founded in love and that he only desires what is good for us.

It is a daily challenge to live according to God's Word. But with fervent prayer and the power of the Holy Spirit, we can walk in obedience and enjoy the blessings that God has in store for us. God can give us the strength we need to resist temptation, avoid forbidden fruit, and keep our fingers where they belong.

I Desire

Lord, I desire to do what is right
And live as righteous in your sight.
Lord, I desire to trust and obey
To serve you faithfully day by day.

Lord, I desire to share your love
And all your blessings from above.
Lord, I desire to know your plan
To do your will the best that I can.

Lord, I desire to turn from my sin,
To be forgiven and cleansed within,
To follow you wherever you lead,
To honor you in thought, word, and deed.

Lord, I desire to praise your name.
Your power and glory I wish to proclaim.
Help me to cling to all that is true
That I may dwell forever with you.

Creation

The mountains declare your majesty.
The ocean reveals your power.
The earth brings forth your goodness.
Your kindness is seen in a flower.

Your greatness shines through the stars in the sky,
And the planets in outer space.
A rainbow glowing in the sky
Reflects your endless grace.

Lord, I sense your nearness
As gentle breezes blow.
Lord, I see your faithfulness
As seasons come and go.

And though I cannot see your face,
Each day I know it's true—
When I look at your creation
I can get a glimpse of you.

Fourth Grade

A word aptly spoken is like apples of gold in settings of silver.

Proverbs 25:11

The year was 1960. South Side Christian School was facing a dilemma as baby boomers filled the crowded classrooms, and there was a shortage of teachers. Two city blocks from the school stood a large, modern church with an empty basement. The decision was made to convert the church basement into a fourth-grade classroom and to assign forty-three students to nine months of education in the available facility.

There was only one teacher who had the emotional and physical fortitude to supervise, control, and educate forty-three active ten-year-olds, and her name was Mrs. Beckman. She was a large woman whose mere presence commanded respect.

I was fortunate to be one of the forty-three students who had the opportunity to experience this unforgettable school year. We adjusted quickly to our unique classroom setting and enjoyed the luxury of spacious living, far removed from bossy sixth-graders and kindergarten babies.

An organized, disciplined teacher, Mrs. Beckman alphabetized everything from library books to coat hooks. Every week she assigned specific duties to a handful of students who were responsible for keeping the classroom neat and orderly. Our textbooks were kept in boxes beneath our wooden chairs, and each of us had a cubby hole where we could store extra belongings.

Mrs. Beckman made us work very hard, but we were often rewarded with an extra long recess. Instead of simply sending us out to play so she could have a much-needed break, Mrs. Beckman slipped on a pair of tennis shoes, hung a whistle around her neck, and joined us for a time of recreation in the church parking lot.

But Mrs. Beckman was more than just a good teacher. She had the creativity and passion of a theatrical director and spent long, laborious hours teaching us musical numbers to perform for our parents, siblings, and friends. We acted out plays and presented musical programs for every seasonal and patriotic event she could think of.

Mrs. Beckman was also sensitive to the emotional needs of her students. She often praised and encouraged those who were shy and insecure and occasionally humbled those who were proud or arrogant. She tried to bring out the best in her students, helping each one discover his or her unique talents and abilities.

One time, she gave us the assignment to write a poem about something we enjoyed doing. I decided to write about a day at our cottage and composed verse after verse of my very first poem. Several days later, Mrs. Beckman stood on her platform, announcing that she had graded the poems.

"I enjoyed reading your poems, class," she said enthusiastically. "Many of them were very good, and someday Crystal is going to be a poet."

Her words flooded my soul with a sense of self-esteem I had never before experienced. The bright red "A" on my paper confirmed my teacher's assessment of my ability and put a smile on my face for the rest of the school year.

I will forever cherish the fond memories of my fourth-grade experience and my wonderful teacher, Mrs. Beckman. The seed she planted deep within me blossomed three decades later when I published *Cracks in the Sidewalk,* my first book of poetry. In April of 1993, Crystal became a poet.

Black Penny Loafers

For the LORD will be your confidence and will keep your foot from being snared.

Proverbs 3:26

I think I spent the entire month of August preparing for my first day of high school. The preparation, however, did not occur at the library, but it began at Boven's Dry Goods Store. Since my fourteen-year-old body could still wear a girl's size twelve, I sewed many of my outfits in order to have teenage fashions.

The hot colors for fall were pink and burgundy. Jumpers were in and so were giant zippers. I found some deep burgundy material, an easy-to-sew pattern, and a big black zipper with a gold ring. I purchased the necessary items and spent several days at our sewing machine creating the perfect outfit for the big day.

After my jumper was finished, I needed to acquire the appropriate accessories. My pink cotton blouse and coffee bean nylons would do, but a new purse and pair of shoes were a must. The boutique shop had a variety of purses from which to choose. I selected a black leather tote with a chunky gold chain, then headed to my favorite shoe store to complete the outfit. My parents were friends with the owner of the store, who often let us take shoes home on approval. The owner wasn't there at the time, but one of the clerks turned out to be very helpful. Walking back and forth over the flat gray carpet convinced me that the black penny loafers fit perfectly; they would be my final purchase.

As the first day of school rapidly approached, I was filled with a mixture of emotions. I was eager to see my friends from junior high and excited by the possibility of making new friends. But would I really fit in? And what about sharing the hallway and cafeteria with those adult seniors?

I awoke at 6:45 that morning, forced myself to eat breakfast, and nervously styled my hair. At least there was one thing I was confident about, and that was my outfit. I zipped up my jumper, put a few necessary items in my new purse, and slipped into my black penny loafers. I rode to school with my big sister, who assured me that I looked very nice.

The first agenda for the day was finding my homeroom. Up a flight of wooden stairs and off to the left was the room where I would begin each day of the entire school year. As I walked into the room and found a seat, I looked around at the other students.

There was a variety of zippered jumpers and lots of burgundy clothing, but no one in the entire room was wearing black penny loafers. Every female foot sported plain burgundy loafers with no slot for the penny.

I spent every class period of the entire day searching for another pair of black penny loafers, but there were none to be found. How could I have been so ignorant? Why didn't the shoe salesman tell me that plain burgundy loafers were the "in thing"? Maybe they didn't have them in my size!

Immediately after school I cleaned the bottom of my shoes, placed them back in the box, and convinced my sister to drive me to the shoe store.

"I need to exchange these," I said to the owner, who happened to be there.

"Is something wrong?" he asked.

"They're just not the right shoe for me," I answered.

"Well then, we'd better find the right shoe for you—and the left one too!" he remarked with his typical dry humor. "I don't want my favorite customer to be unhappy."

"Do you have anything in burgundy, perhaps without the penny part?" I asked hopefully.

"Let me take a look," he replied as he disappeared through an open doorway.

It seemed like hours before he finally emerged with shoe box in hand.

"Is this what you're looking for?" he asked as he held up one of the shoes.

"Yes," I said, with a sigh of relief. "Those are perfect!"

I exchanged shoe boxes with the owner and went home happy.

The next day, I went to school wearing my navy blue skirt and red cardigan sweater—another popular look. But with added confidence, I walked out the door in my plain burgundy loafers.

As a grown woman, I still enjoy being in style, but my confidence comes from who I am in Jesus Christ rather than from my wardrobe. The Bible speaks of an outfit that will give us confidence for our daily lives, and it's always in style.

Ephesians 6:13–17 instructs us to put on the full armor of God, so we will be able to stand firm against evil. We must gird our loins with truth and wear the breastplate of righteousness and the helmet of salvation. We can also protect ourselves by carrying the shield of faith and the sword of the Spirit. And to complete our outfit, on our feet we must wear the gospel of peace. I wonder if that comes in a plain burgundy loafer?

Little Angels

Trust in the LORD with all your heart and lean not on your own understanding; in all your ways acknowledge him, and he will make your paths straight.

Proverbs 3:5–6

I didn't spend four years in college so I could get knots out of shoelaces, mix Kool-Aid, and wipe slimy noses!" I grumbled to myself as I pulled into the parking lot of Little Angels Nursery School on a warm September morning. It was my first "real" job since earning my bachelor's degree, and I was not happy. I preferred older kids who had brains and I wanted to teach math, not Dr. Seuss. Unfortunately, it was my one and only job offer and I had bills to pay.

To make matters worse, I didn't even get a teaching position. The only opening the preschool had was a teacher's aide position at minimum wage. I could have skipped four years of college, saved a lot of money, and still been qualified for this lowly job.

My first day was memorable. One of the boy angels wet his pants, and a female angel discovered a bottle of red nail polish and used it to decorate her new white sweater. I spent most of the day cleaning paint spills, wiping yellow spots off toilet seats, and getting Susie's bubble gum out of Brian's hair. As I collapsed on the sofa that evening, I decided I would continue searching for a job until I found something that I deserved.

Days, weeks, and months passed by, and soon the little angels were sprinkling silver glitter on cotton-ball mountains and gluing Fruit Loops onto green paper Christmas trees. I was still getting knots out of shoelaces, mixing Kool-Aid, and wiping slimy noses but had somehow lost interest in finding another job. I'm not sure if it was when Joey told me his dad was a "buttographer," or the time Stevie asked me to marry him, but somewhere along the way, the little angels stole my heart.

As I got acquainted with these three- and four-year-old creatures, I realized that not only were they sweet, sensitive, and caring individuals, they were also bright, creative, and eager to learn. Their innocence and naiveté added humor to every situation and made me wish I could somehow recapture their paradigm. My fascination with these little ones continued to grow, and I cherished every opportunity I had to interact with them. Since this was an area of education I never would have pursued on my own, I realized that God, in his infinite wisdom, had led me to Little Angels Nursery School so I could discover the career for which I was created.

The following September I filled a teacher's position that had become available and also enrolled in an early childhood program at the University of Michigan. I continued to teach preschool for several years while taking evening and summer classes.

Even though my professional teaching career came to an end with the birth of my first child, I continued to apply what I had learned while raising my three children.

When my youngest child started school, I once again had a few hours to pursue some personal goals. I was overwhelmed with a desire to write for children and began to move in that direction. A children's book editor asked me if I had any experience with preschool children or if I had ever studied early childhood development. It was then that I fully recognized God's divine plan unfolding before me. Little did I know, on that warm September morning, that God was preparing me to be a preschool teacher, mother, and eventually a children's book author. I am thankful that even when my attitude needed an adjustment, God was faithful in guiding and directing my life according to his will.

My years at Little Angels Nursery School were truly a blessing. I discovered the joy of teaching young children, while they taught me much about life. I know I will always have a special love in my heart for little children—even if they need their noses wiped.

You and I

When I don't know the way,
you direct me.
When I disobey,
you correct me.
When I make mistakes,
and lack what it takes,
by your grace, Lord,
you perfect me.

When I'm discouraged,
you cheer me.
When I cry for help,
you hear me.
When I need a friend
on whom I can depend,
Lord, I know
you are always near me.

By your mercy
you forgave me.
When I was lost,
you saved me.
You paid the price
with the blood of Christ.
Salvation is what
you gave me.

Mother's Peace

And the peace of God, which transcends all understanding, will guard your hearts and your minds in Christ Jesus.

Philippians 4:7

With twelve boys and two girls, it was the fourth-grade Sunday school class nobody wanted to teach. Every week I read the plea in the bulletin. I was twenty-three and naïve, and I thought I could handle the challenge. I was wrong. I wanted to quit after my first week, but my husband, Bob, convinced me to give it another try and offered to help. It turned out to be a winning combination. Though I did most of the teaching, Bob motivated the children with competitive games and Bible trivia and somehow managed to keep them in their seats for fifty-five minutes. The children responded positively to our leadership, and we had fourteen sets of grateful parents, not to mention an elated superintendent.

We had every imaginable type of child in our class. There was Doug, the talkative one who desired to be the center of attention. There was Benny, who never said a word. There was Kevin, who wanted to answer all of the questions. And there was Josh, the class clown. The two girls found refuge in each other and could hold their own in spite of being outnumbered. I hate to admit that we had a favorite student, but we did. His name was Greg, and he was as close to perfect as any ten-year-old boy could be. He raised his hand when he wanted to speak. He was always on time, always polite, always knew his memory verse, and was never mean to the other kids. We decided that if we ever had a son, we would want him to be like Greg.

We taught the class for almost a year, until Bob's graduation brought us back to our hometown. We found another couple to replace us and were confident that the class was in good hands.

A few weeks after we moved, I got a call from the superintendent, informing me that Greg had been struck by a car and killed while riding his bike to Bible school. My shock was replaced by anger, and for several days I didn't open my Bible or pray. *How could God do this?* I wondered.

I wrote a letter to Greg's parents and slipped it inside a sympathy card, which I sent in the mail. A week later, I received a call from Greg's mother. She perceived my anger through the letter and called to give me words of hope and encouragement. She shared with me that she felt the presence of the Lord as soon as she was told about the accident. She said that Greg's body was so severely injured in the accident that his death was an answer to prayer. She also asked me to pray for the young woman who was driving the car, as she was not a Christian.

After we hung up, I was ashamed of my attitude. If Greg's mother was at peace with God, who was I to question him? It was then that I accepted the promise of God to give us peace in the midst of our storms—peace that surpasses all human understanding.

Though I may never know why God chose to take Greg home at such a young age, I have peace in knowing that God is sovereign, that his ways are not my ways, and that he is in control.

When problems overwhelm us
And trials come our way,
When life is so confusing
That it's difficult to pray,
Trust in God's great promises—
His love will never cease.
He alone can heal our pain
And fill our hearts with peace.

$Two-Fifty

A slight misunderstanding can be emotionally demanding.

When Bob finished his education and started a business, we began the next chapter of our lives. Money was tight, and we had an agreement that we would not spend it without each other's approval. I had been teaching preschool for three years (not a high-paying occupation) and hoped to find a similar teaching position near our apartment, since we would be sharing our only car. A colleague informed me that I could file an application with a central office to which most preschool administrators had access. I did some investigating and shared the opportunity with Bob.

"For two-fifty, I can have an application on file at the early childhood central office," I explained to him. "With my experience and education, I should have a good chance if there are any jobs available."

I was surprised that Bob wasn't more enthused.

"I don't know," was all he responded as he shrugged his shoulders.

I interpreted his response as a way of keeping me from getting my hopes up. I knew it was a long shot, but I felt it was worth pursuing.

The following week I was ecstatic when I received a phone call from the director of a preschool only a few miles from our home. She wanted me to stop by for an interview and said she was eager to meet with me.

"How did she find out about you?" Bob asked in bewilderment when I shared the good news.

"I put my application in at the central office—the deal I told you about last week," I explained.

"You mean you spent two hundred and fifty dollars just to fill out an application?" he asked in horror.

"Noooooo," I slowly replied, finally understanding the whole misunderstanding. "I spent two dollars and fifty cents."

My husband looked thoroughly relieved, yet somewhat exhausted, by this emotional episode.

"Listen, dear," he said firmly but kindly, "the next time you want to spend two dollars and fifty cents for something you feel is worth it, please don't ask me—just do it!"

Miscommunications are common in our human relationships. Sometimes they are harmless, but they can often be the cause of frustration, confusion, or disappointment. I'm thankful that my relationship with God isn't like that. He understands my prayers, my concerns, and even my thoughts—sometimes better than I do! With God, the communication lines are always open, and there are no misunderstandings.

And by the way—I got the job!

Seasons

Lord, I love the summer days
When robins sing their songs of praise.
A clear blue sky, a bright warm sun,
Children who laugh and play and run.

Lord, I love the autumn trees
With orange and red and yellow leaves.
Quiet days and chilly nights,
And critters with hungry appetites.

In winter your splendor sparkles the land.
You dress the earth with the touch of your hand.
A soft white blanket covers the ground
As snowflakes gently float all around.

Springtime gives new life to earth.
Flowers awake and the creatures give birth.
All of creation is fresh and new,
Giving honor and praise and glory to you.

As months go by and seasons change,
And things in nature rearrange,
Your power, love, and majesty
Are visible for all to see.

You Gave Me Eyes

You gave me eyes so I can see
The beautiful things you've created for me.
Help me to see all that is good
And focus my eyes on the things that I should.

You gave me ears so I can hear
The bluebird's morning song of cheer.
Help me to listen to all that is true
And hear only things that bring glory to you.

You gave me lips so I can praise
And worship you in so many ways.
Help me to speak words that are kind
That through my lips your light may shine.

You gave me a mind so I can know
The meaning of life on earth here below.
Help my thoughts to be holy and right
And always pleasing in your sight.

You gave me a life so I can live
In service to you for the blessings you give.
Help me to honor you every day
To follow your will, to trust and obey.

The New House

I have learned the secret of being content in any and every situation.

Philippians 4:12b

*a*fter living in two-bedroom apartments for the first five years of our marriage, I was overjoyed when we were finally able to purchase a house. Not only was it our first real house, but we were also moving into a new development where the houses were just being built. We picked out a wooded lot, chose the walk-out ranch floor plan, and began the exciting process of building our first home.

We only had one child but hoped to have more children in the near future and planned on "growing" into our home. We decided to finish the areas of the house that were a necessity and leave the rest of the house unfinished until we needed more space.

The first few weeks of living in our new home were total luxury. I felt I had everything I needed—except a washer and dryer. It was very inconvenient to go to the laundromat with a two-year-old child. I finally convinced Bob that if we bought a washer and dryer, I'd be all set and wouldn't need one more thing.

We bought the washer and dryer, and they were wonderful. With joyful appreciation, I regularly tossed bathroom towels and teddy bear sheets into the washing machine while my son Robby sat at the kitchen counter eating macaroni and cheese. In the afternoons, I'd wash and fold another load while he took his nap. Life was good and I was happy.

But after a few months, I got tired of stepping on Play-Doh crumbs in the kitchen and tripping over fire engines in the living room. If we could just finish the playroom, I could keep most of the toys in there and shut the door when we had company.

So we finished the toy room. And that was wonderful for a while, until I felt we needed to finish the extra bathroom. And as long as we were at it, why not finish the guest room? And if we finished the extra room in the basement, we could use it for an office so our papers wouldn't pile up on the kitchen counter. And we should probably get air-conditioning before summer since meteorologists had predicted a hot one. And I *really* needed an upright freezer for the garage since I couldn't possibly pack all of our frozen items in the little freezer in our refrigerator.

Then, one day, it dawned on me that no matter how many rooms we finished or how many appliances we owned, there would always be something more that I felt we needed. In Ecclesiastes 5:10, we read, "Whoever loves money never has money enough; whoever loves wealth is never satisfied with his income. This too is meaningless."

I realized through this experience that satisfaction can never be obtained through material possessions. In Philippians 4:11–12, the apostle Paul says, "I have learned to be content whatever the circumstances. I know what it is to be in need, and I know what it is to have plenty. I have learned the secret of being content in any and every situation, whether well fed or hungry, whether living in plenty or in want."

Paul's secret to contentment was his relationship with God and his purpose in life. Paul's goal was to serve the Lord and preach the gospel. He trusted God to provide for his needs and, whether he had much or little, he was satisfied.

There is nothing wrong with having a nice home and material possessions, as long as our heart's desire is to serve the Lord. When our focus is on who we are in Christ rather than what we have on earth, contentment is an achievable goal. Our eternal possessions will bring fulfillment and satisfaction, while our earthly possessions will leave us wanting just a little bit more.

Counting My Blessings

In counting my blessings
I need to include:
clean air to breathe,
water and food,
children to teach,
babies to love,
a warm cozy house,
and angels above.

In counting my blessings
I must think of these:
a peaceful sunset,
a warm gentle breeze,
a fresh summer rain,
a starlit night,
and strong little arms
that hug me so tight.

In counting my blessings
these will be there:
friends in my life,
and people that care,
places to worship,
freedom to pray,
and wisdom from God
day after day.

In counting my blessings
it's easy to see,
that the Lord must care
very deeply for me.

Dwell on These Things

Lord, help me dwell
    on things that I should;
    things that are lovely
    and things that are good.
Whatever is noble,
    whatever is true,
    whatever brings honor
    and glory to you.

Whatever is excellent
    or worthy of praise,
Lord, help me dwell on these
    all of my days.
Though trials may come,
    my worries will cease,
And my life will be filled
    with comfort and peace.

Based on Philippians 4:8–9

Fill Me with Your Spirit, Lord

Fill me with your Spirit, Lord,
That I may be patient and kind.
Help me to share your love and joy,
And bless me with peace of mind.

Fill me with goodness and gentleness
That I may treat others that way.
Fill me with your Spirit, Lord,
That I may be faithful each day.

Help me to live in self-control
In all that I say and do,
That through your Spirit I may live
A life that is pleasing to you.

Based on Galatians 5:22

A Mother's Prayer

My gracious heavenly Father,
Please hear me as I pray.
I come to you on bended knee
And ask of you today,
To give me wisdom, strength, and love
To raise my children for you,
That they might love and honor you
In everything they do.

I ask that you'll watch over them
Throughout their childhood years.
Protect them as they run and play
And calm their childish fears.
And when they reach their teenage years
I pray that they'll be strong,
To stand up to temptation
And turn away from wrong.

I pray that they would read your Word
And talk with you each day,
So they will know your perfect will
And follow in your way.
I ask that you would be their guide
As they begin to date.
Help them choose, dear Lord, I pray,
A loving, godly mate.

And when they're blessed with little ones
I pray that they may too
Have the wisdom, strength, and love
To raise their children for you.

Bible Study

Delight yourself in the LORD and he will give you the desires of your heart.

Psalm 37:4

*a*fter the birth of our second son, caring for Robby and Scott consumed most of my time and energy. Though I believe that raising children is a full-time ministry, I was longing for another area of service that would still allow me to be the mother I desired to be. Making a commitment to teach Sunday school every week was out of the question, but I didn't know what else I could do. I finally gave it over to God and decided that he would show me his plan. The next day I received an unexpected phone call from a youth director in our area.

"I hope I'm not calling too early," he said, in an attempt to apologize for the morning call.

"Not around here," I assured him. "My kids are always up before the sun."

"The reason for the call," he continued, "is that I have a small group of girls who want an after-school Bible study. I don't have a leader or a place to have it, and I don't know why, but for some reason you came to my mind."

"They can have it here and I'll lead it," I replied matter-of-factly.

Silence.

"Hello, Rick, are you still there?"

"Yes, I'm still here," he answered. "It's just that I'm overwhelmed by your response. You are an answer to prayer."

"No," I corrected him, "*you* are an answer to prayer."

As I explained to him my desire to minister to someone, somewhere, we were both in awe of how God worked everything out.

For an entire school year, a handful of teenage girls came over every Monday after school to talk, pray, and study God's Word. A ten-year-old neighbor girl enjoyed playing with my boys for a dollar an hour *in my home,* while I enjoyed fellowship with enthusiastic teens *in my home*. God knew the desires of my heart and provided me with the perfect opportunity.

It was a blessing for me to see the girls work out their problems and grow in their faith. They usually stayed well beyond the designated departure time and often helped with dinner and caring for the boys. Two of them became regular baby-sitters, and one girl became a lifelong friend.

I believe that God can use us regardless of our circumstances. We are not all called to be teachers or leaders; there are many areas of service where Christian women are desperately needed. If you have a desire to be involved in a ministry, simply ask God for his direction and let him know the desires of your heart. And don't be surprised when the phone rings.

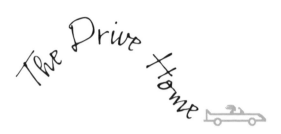

The Drive Home

For he will command his angels concerning you to guard you in all your ways.

Psalm 91:11

The winding mountain road was dark and quiet as the two men headed home after a weekend of extreme skiing. Their middle-aged muscles reminded them that they were no longer young, but they had proven to themselves and each other that they could still ski the black-diamond slopes with the best of the best.

It was not out of willful defiance but a desire to reach home that encouraged the driver to exceed the speed limit. The two wanted to get home by midnight so their exhausted bodies could collapse in their own warm, comfortable beds. They were about an hour from the city when a red flashing light in the rearview mirror caught their attention.

"So much for getting home by midnight," the driver muttered to his friend as the officer walked toward their car.

"May I see your driver's license, please?" the officer asked politely.

"Yes, sir," the driver responded.

"I know the roads are lonely tonight," the officer stated in a kind, fatherly voice, "but I want you to get home safely. Please slow it down a bit."

He spent a few moments in his cruiser, handed the driver a written warning, then disappeared into the darkness.

"That only set us back nine minutes," the passenger said to the driver. "We'll still make it home in good time."

The two men safely continued their journey to the city but were greeted by more red flashing lights when they finally arrived.

"Can't get through here," an officer informed the men as they stopped at a barrier in the road. "There's been a bad accident—some drunk driver crossed the line and smashed head-on into an oncoming car. Just happened about nine minutes ago."

The men gave each other a sober glance, both thinking the same thing—*what if?* They slowly turned their car around and quietly traveled home on another route.

When my husband returned home from Colorado the next day, he shared his spine-chilling story with me. He was the passenger, and his friend, who lived in Denver, was the driver. My mind soon began to wonder: Was the officer who stopped them really an officer, or was he an angel in disguise, sent by God to spare my husband and his friend from a tragic accident?

When I went to bed that night, I prayed for the families whose lives had been forever changed by a senseless accident and thanked God for returning my husband home safely.

I also thanked God for the officer whose divine intervention may have spared the life of my husband and his friend. Though I wasn't sure of the officer's name, I think it was either Michael or Gabriel.

Just Call Me Martha

I meditate on your precepts and consider your ways. I delight in your decrees; I will not neglect your word.

Psalm 119:15–16

*a*s mothers of young children know, it is difficult to find time for daily devotions. A typical day consists of tending to the needs of little ones, and uninterrupted slices of time are rare. When Robby and Scott were preschoolers, I tried to make a regular practice of spending fifteen minutes each day reading a few Bible verses and praying to God. Since I am a morning person, I knew that if I didn't take time for devotions before noon, it probably wouldn't happen that day. Fortunately, my boys were *Sesame Street* fans and would usually be mesmerized long enough for me to accomplish my spiritual goal at some time during the sixty-minute program.

One particular morning, I was especially busy, since some women from church were coming over for a meeting. Not only did I need to do the usual tasks of making beds and emptying the diaper pail, I also wanted to wipe fingerprints off the end tables, sweep up the Cheerios, and plug in the coffeepot.

As Robby and Scott were being entertained by Big Bird and Snuffleupagus, I decided it was the perfect time to get the house ready for my guests. *Isn't this the time you usually spend with me?* I heard someone say—not out loud, but somewhere in my head.

"But, God," I replied in defense, "these are my friends from *church,* and I'm practicing hospitality, which isn't even my spiritual gift. Doesn't that count?"

It was no use. I knew I would have no peace of mind unless I stopped for a few moments and had my daily devotions. I reached for my Bible and slipped my index finger between the pages that were already separated by my "World's Greatest Mom" bookmark. I began reading at the place where I had stopped the day before.

The passage I happened to read that morning was from Luke 10:38–42, which tells the story of Jesus at the home of his friends, Mary and Martha. Martha was busy in the kitchen preparing and serving food, while Mary sat at the feet of Jesus, listening to him speak. Martha was not pleased with her sister's actions.

"Lord, don't you care that my sister has left me to do the work by myself?" Martha asks Jesus. "Tell her to help me!"

Jesus' reply was not quite what Martha expected.

"Martha, Martha," the Lord answered, "you are worried and upset about many things, but only one thing is needed. Mary has chosen what is better."

I may as well have read the verse using *my* name instead of Martha's, since I knew God was talking directly to me. As I closed my Bible, I was thankful that I had stopped being Martha for just a little while so I could listen to the Lord and spend some time with him.

In the following minutes, I managed to get rid of the fingerprints and Cheerios, and the coffee was ready when my friends arrived. As we gathered around the kitchen table, I suggested that we begin our meeting with a few Bible verses and a time of prayer.

"I'm going to read a passage from Luke 10," I announced. "It's something I read recently, and I'd like to share it with you."

Marathon Mom

I woke today at six o'clock,
I felt like it was three.
My eyes are red, my hair's a mess,
I have no energy.
My baby has a runny nose,
my toddler has the flu.
My six-year-old has school today;
he cannot find his shoe.

Another pair of training pants
has just been flushed away.
I'll have to call a plumber.
Lord, get me through this day!
There's clothing in the laundry room
I don't have time to fold.
The dishes piled in the sink
have started growing mold.

Could it be coincidence?
I don't believe in chance,
but every time the doorbell rings,
my daughter wets her pants.
And when I use the telephone
to give my friend a call,
someone finds a crayon
and decorates the wall.

I cleaned the house just yesterday,
Lord, it isn't fair—
the fingerprints have reappeared
and toys are everywhere.
My husband just gave me a call,
he says he's working late—
so go ahead and feed the kids,
he'll be home after eight.

After two more storybooks,
and one last hug and kiss,
the children are all tucked in bed.
I sense a quiet bliss.
Indulging in my quiet time,
I rest and pray and think.
Then I hear a tender voice say,
"Mom, I need a drink."
Lord, I know these little ones
are precious gifts from you.
Give me patience, strength, and love,
each day, to make it through.

Letters from Grandma

Children's children are a crown to the aged, and parents are the pride of their children.

Proverbs 17:6

When Audrey, my friend's mother, was in her seventies, she decided to purchase a computer and learn how to use it. For several decades she had been using time-consuming methods to record the petitions and praises of her prayer group. The computer would enable her to accomplish the task with ease and speed. The computer soon became her "friend," and she began using it for more than keeping records for her prayer group.

One day, Audrey decided to write letters to each of her fourteen grandchildren and three great-grandchildren. The response was so positive that she determined to make letter-writing a regular event. Each month, Audrey spent a morning at her computer composing the two-page letters. She shared delightful tales from her childhood—like the time she "borrowed" a nickel from the family tithe box so she could buy a candy bar. She recalled how her conscience made her so miserable that she finally confessed the sin to her father. She shared interesting information about extended family members and always included a bit of humor. In one letter, she told about the time a man got up in church and announced the singing of her favorite hymn. As she joined him in song, she soon realized that she was the only one in the audience singing. The man was a guest soloist and was not expecting a duet!

In every letter Audrey included a riddle, a proverb, a Scripture verse, and a prayer.

She sometimes shared a witty poem and often enclosed a published story or article she found meaningful. Audrey would list the dates and names of cousins who were celebrating birthdays or anniversaries that month. "Isn't it nice to know that your cousins will be praying for you on your special day?" she would ask, as a way of reminding them to pray for one another.

Audrey would often "tease" the kids about the contents of future letters. "Next month," she would write, "I will tell you about something that happened to me on my way to school, and I will tell you something about Aunt Trudy."

The grandchildren and great-grandchildren eagerly anticipated the monthly letters. They enjoyed the wonderful stories and appreciated the personalized paragraph in each letter. Every month they were comforted and inspired by Audrey's closing words, "God loves you and so do I. I pray God's very best for you. I pray for God's guidance and protection in whatever you do and wherever you go." They also appreciated the one-dollar bills she tucked inside before sealing the envelopes.

On June 30, 1999, Audrey sat at her computer and composed the letters as she did each month. She mailed them promptly that day, knowing they would be transported over various county and state lines into the mailboxes of her fourteen grandchildren and three great-grandchildren. The next day, Audrey went for a walk and busied herself with her usual daily activities. In the evening, she rested on her sofa, reading the day's mail and scanning magazines for interesting articles. She dozed off for a few moments, as she often did, then quietly slipped into the presence of her heavenly Father.

Through misty eyes, the grandchildren and great-grandchildren read the final words of wisdom, encouragement, and humor from their eighty-four-year-old grandmother. The proverb she chose for this month was, "Don't put off until tomorrow what could and should be done today." And, instead of including a one-dollar bill, she placed a twenty-dollar bill in each envelope. Did Audrey know that she didn't have another "tomorrow" on earth? No one but God knows for sure.

The letters from Grandma will be cherished forever by the grandchildren and great-grandchildren who received them each month. Even though she is no longer with them, her words of inspiration and encouragement will continue to bless them for many years to come. Perhaps someday they, too, will compose letters to their grandchildren and great-grandchildren—maybe on something that has not yet been invented.

The Vintage Woman

She speaks with words of wisdom
For life has taught her much.
Charm and grace adorn her,
There is softness in her touch.

The tales she tells are bittersweet,
A blend of joy and pain.
For as her loved ones pass away,
Her memories still remain.

She talks to God throughout the day
For he's become her friend,
The one she can depend on
Time and time again.

She reaches out to those in need,
She's quick to lend a hand.
Many share their problems
For she seems to understand.

She labors daily for the Lord,
For heaven is her goal.
And though her body's aging
She has strength within her soul.

Her days on earth are numbered
For life goes by so fast.
And all that she has done for Christ
Has value that will last.

The Camera

This is the message we have heard from him and declare to you: God is light; in him there is no darkness at all.

1 John 1:5

When Robby was four years old, one of his favorite toys was a red-and-white plastic Viewmaster that he called his camera. It was one of my favorite toys as well, because it kept him occupied for hours. He had a shoe box full of cardboard discs with picture frames of Bugs Bunny, Snoopy, and G.I. Joe. With each click of the knob, the scene would magically change, portraying tales of conflict, humor, and triumph. Every birthday and Christmas gave us an opportunity to add to his collection of cartoon entertainment and renew his interest in this priceless toy.

Then, one afternoon, my son came to me with a horrified look on his face. "My camera is broken!" he said, as he handed me his toy.

I held the Viewmaster toward the light and placed my eyes on the lens. "It's working just fine," I assured him as I put it back in his dimpled hands.

He peered through the lens and again wailed, "It's broken, Mommy; I can't see anything!"

I realized that he couldn't see the picture because he wasn't holding it toward the light.

"You need to hold it like this," I said, as I demonstrated the correct technique.

"Oh, now I see it!" he replied with a sigh of relief.

My son's inability to see the picture reminded me of people who live their lives in darkness. In John 8:12, Jesus says, "I am the light of the world. Whoever follows me will never walk in darkness, but will have the light of life."

When people choose to "do their own thing" or "go their own way" they will soon stumble in the darkness of life, not knowing which way to turn. Those who choose, however, to have a personal relationship with Jesus Christ and live in daily fellowship with him will gain insight into the purpose of their lives and discover God's wonderful plan for them. When we fix our eyes on Jesus, we will see things more clearly. Get the picture?

> There's no need to stumble and lose your way,
> Or live in the darkness day after day.
> Trust the Lord Jesus and walk in the light.
> He'll show you each day the path that is right.
> With eyes fixed on Jesus you'll clearly see
> A colorful picture that's bright as can be.

Greeters

> Do not forget to entertain strangers, for by so doing some people have entertained angels without knowing it.
>
> Hebrews 13:2

When our children were young, it worked best for our family to arrive at church early on Sunday morning. We could get a parking spot close to the door on cold rainy days and sit in a pew toward the front of church where our children seemed to behave their best.

One of the ushers noticed our faithfulness in arriving early and asked if we would consider being greeters. He promised to reserve our desired pew while we offered a warm smile and a handshake to the arriving congregation. We thought it sounded like fun and agreed to greet as a family one Sunday each month.

Since we attend a large church, we had the opportunity to meet new people as well as welcome familiar faces. One morning a young family asked us for directions as soon as they arrived. "We are visiting," they informed us, "and we don't have any idea where to go."

When they said they wanted to stay for Sunday school as well as the worship service, we were somewhat perplexed as to how we would explain where each of their three children had to go.

"I have an idea," announced my husband. "We are going to adopt you for the morning. Meet us here after the service and we will take your kids to their Sunday school rooms. After Sunday school is over, we will help you round up your kids, and you can be on your way."

At first they hesitated, not wanting to impose. But when we told them jokingly that there was a possibility they might never see their children again, they finally agreed.

We ended up having a wonderful time with the visiting family, and they admitted that they couldn't have survived the morning without our help. We exchanged phone numbers and addresses and expressed our desire to see each other again.

The following week we received a letter from the family, telling us that they were missionaries in search of a home church. They expressed their appreciation for making them feel welcome and shared that they had decided to choose our church. I was humbled to think that our family had played a small part in helping them reach their decision.

There are many people who feel their area of service is not that important. We often think the teachers, preachers, and music directors have the most important positions. The apostle Paul tells us, "Just as each of us has one body with many members, and these members do not all have the same function, so in Christ we who are many form one body, and each member belongs to all the others. We have different gifts, according to the grace given us" (Rom. 12:4–6a).

It's not our gifts or abilities that are important to God, it's whether or not we use them that matters. Making coffee for the visitors' reception, washing the communion cups, or changing diapers in the nursery are just as important as the areas of ministry that are more visible. If someone doesn't see to it that the sound system is working, what good is the pastor's message? If the bulletins don't get typed and printed, how can the members be informed? And if there are no greeters at the doors, how will a visiting family know where to go?

For many Sundays our family enjoyed the opportunity to function in the body of Christ by welcoming members and visitors. It's a blessing to know that we not only shook many hands but we also touched a few lives.

Did God Choose to Use You?

Did God choose to use you
To help someone today?
Did God choose to use you
In some special way?

Did you say the right words?
Did you do a good deed?
Did you kindly respond
To a sister in need?

Did you teach a young child?
Did you show that you care?
Did somebody say,
"You're an answer to prayer"?

Then give thanks to God—
Give the glory to him,
That he chose to use you
In spite of your sin.

You may not be perfect
Or gifted or smart.
But God can still use you,
If he's in your heart.

And when you allow
His Spirit to come in,
He may choose to use you
Again and again.

My Birthday

"What do you want for your birthday?"
My children asked one day.
I didn't have to stop and think,
I answered right away.

"I'd like a house that's nice and clean,
And children that love each other.
I'd like the laundry to wash itself
Without the help of a mother.

"I'd like the meals to be easy to make
And always taste delicious.
And after our elegant dinner is through,
A little help with the dishes.

"I'd like to soak in a bubble bath
And never answer the phone.
I'd like to listen to Mozart
And have an evening alone.

"But if it isn't possible
To give me all of this,
Just tell me that you love me,
And give me a birthday kiss."

Breakfast in Bed

My children made me breakfast in bed—
The finest meal I've ever been fed.

The toast was dry and rather burned,
I think the pancake didn't get turned.

They dropped the oatmeal on the floor,
Scooped it up and made some more.

The scrambled eggs were somewhat raw,
But I didn't really mind at all.

The orange juice tasted slightly sour,
My children slaved for over an hour.

The coffee was poured in a dinosaur mug,
My breakfast was served with a kiss and a hug.

There's no better way to start the day
Than breakfast in bed on a plastic tray.

My Words

My words can sing your praises, Lord.
My words can say a prayer.
My words can say encouraging things
To let others know that I care.

Give me words of comfort, Lord,
For those who are distressed.
Give me words of hope and praise
For those who have done their best.

Help my words to always be kind,
Help my words to be true.
Help me to think before I speak
So my words are pleasing to you.

And if my loved ones say to me,
"Your words do not delight us,"
Give me, for a day or two,
A case of laryngitis.

The Perfect Woman

The perfect woman eats a gourmet dinner
    while her waistline keeps getting thinner
    and thinner.
The perfect woman has long, silky hair
    that's easy to style—just wash and wear.

Her skin is smooth, it always looks great,
    and she never needs to exfoliate.
The perfect woman wears stylish clothes
    and rarely powders her feminine nose.

Her lashes are thick, she has dazzling eyes,
    she is beautiful, charming, graceful, and wise.
The perfect woman—no man could resist,
    but take heart, dear friends,
    she doesn't exist!

The Telephone Pole

Gossip is anything that goes in one ear and over the back fence.

Uncle Ben's Quote Book

I had a friend with whom I shared almost everything over the telephone. I could brag about my kids, complain about my neighbor, or talk about my latest project. She was a good listener and fun to talk to. Sometimes, however, our conversations contained non-edifying information about mutual friends and acquaintances. I never thought of our confidential verbal exchanges as gossip, but one day I realized that they were certainly leaning in that direction.

I determined that, with God's help, I was going to be more careful in what I shared with my friend over the telephone. I once heard some good advice from a speaker: "Don't say anything behind a person's back that you wouldn't say if she were there." I decided that I would try to put that rule into practice and carefully guard my tongue.

For several weeks things went very well. Then one day at church, I had an unpleasant encounter with a nursery worker. I was insulted and offended, and I fumed about it for days. I desperately wanted to call my friend to explain the whole ugly scene. I needed someone to tell me that I was right and the other person was wrong. I finally convinced myself that I would be doing the right thing by telling my friend, because if I didn't tell her, the same thing could happen to her. It was my duty as a friend to protect her from being insulted and offended.

With bold determination, I picked up the receiver and quickly pushed the numbers on my telephone keypad that would have her phone ringing in a matter of seconds. Hearing nothing in my receiver, I surmised that I must have dialed too quickly and made a second attempt. Still nothing. I tried one more time, then realized that my phone was not working.

As I walked past the living room on my way to another extension, I noticed a utility truck in my driveway and a telephone pole lying across my front yard.

"What's the problem?" I asked a repairman as I anxiously appeared in the driveway.

"No problem, ma'am," he replied. "Just need to replace this old pole before it falls down and does some serious damage. Your phone will be working by dinnertime. Sorry for the inconvenience."

As I went back into the house, a Bible verse came to mind. "No temptation has seized you except what is common to man. And God is faithful; he will not let you be tempted beyond what you can bear. But when you are tempted, he will also provide a way out so that you can stand up under it" (1 Cor. 10:13).

In my moment of weakness, God provided a way out, so I could not give in to temptation. By dinnertime, my phone was alive and well, but I had changed my mind about sharing the unpleasant incident with my friend. She didn't need me to protect her against this person, and this person didn't need me to spread unkind things about her to others.

The temptation to gossip is something that most of us live with from day to day, and it's often difficult to stand up to the temptation. But now when I am tempted to gossip, I not only think of the sound advice I heard from that speaker several years ago, I also remember the telephone pole lying in my front yard.

Little White Lie

It started out as a little white lie,
no harm intended—
just let it pass by.
But the little white lie
soon needed a cover,
so one little lie
quickly led to another.

The little white lie
continued to grow,
but certainly nobody
needed to know.
Then after a while
came the time to explain,
as one little lie
caused a great deal of pain.

Friends were deceived
and people were hurt.
The little white lie
became covered with dirt.
A jumbled up, fumbled up,
nice little mess,
with wounds that go deep
even though you confess.

How did it happen?
Where did it start?
These little white lies
can tear you apart.
But this sort of thing
will not happen to you.
If you're careful to speak
only words that are true.

Watch Your Step

Cleanse me with hyssop, and I will be clean; wash me, and I will be whiter than snow.

Psalm 51:7

As I walked out of church on a beautiful Sunday morning in March, I inhaled the fresh spring air and squinted from the blinding rays of the brilliant sun. The birds were cheerfully welcoming the springlike weather, and chunky piles of snow were shrinking before my eyes. After months of exposure to traffic, shovels, and plows, the snow had lost the innocent beauty of freshly fallen flakes. The melting snow piles created tiny rippling rivers that traveled rapidly across the pavement, disappearing into strategically located drains. The exiting churchgoers were walking cautiously to their awaiting cars, attempting to avoid unwanted contact with the earthly elements.

An adorable toddler wobbled ahead of me on the sidewalk, proudly holding on to her daddy's hand. Her white eyelet bonnet, navy blue woolen coat, and shiny black patent leather shoes made her look as though she had just stepped out of a page from the JCPenney catalog. As we continued down the sidewalk, I noticed a small pile of mud, slush, and a few other mushy ingredients slightly to the right of our path. The adorable angel noticed it too. I smiled as I watched her deliberately stretch her chubby little leg to the right, in order to sink her tiny patent leather shoe smack dab in the center of the pile. The temptation was more than she could bear.

My heart was touched by what I witnessed next. The father lovingly picked up his child, wiped her off, and set her back on the sidewalk with the messy pile behind them. This little incident reminded me of my relationship with my heavenly Father. Even when I am walking hand in hand with him, it is impossible to live a life that is free from sin. But if I confess my sin, my Father will pick me up, wipe me clean, and set me back on the path of life with the mess behind me.

Forgiveness is a merciful gift of love from God. We don't deserve it, but he offers it to us unconditionally through his Son, Jesus Christ. It is comforting to know that when we mess up our lives, the blood of Jesus Christ can wash away our sins and make us righteous before him.

I know that I will never be able to live a perfect life on Earth, but I can try, each day, to hold on to my Father's hand and watch out for messy piles along the way.

> As you walk along on the journey of life,
> Beware of the dangers you'll find.
> Hold on to your heavenly Father's hand
> And leave all the dangers behind.

I Will Always Love You

I will always love you
No matter what you do.
You'll always be my child,
I'll take good care of you.

Even when you disobey,
Although it makes me sad,
A mother loves her child
Through the good times and the bad.

That is how the Lord loves us
Each and every day—
Not only when we please him,
But also when we stray.

He loves us as his children,
And even when we sin,
His loving arms are open wide
To let us try again.

God's love is everlasting,
His love is strong and true.
His love is like a mother's love,
He cares for me and you.

Yesterday and Today

Yesterday you heard my prayer.
Today I know you're always there.

Yesterday you spoke to me.
Today I listen carefully.

Yesterday you showed your plan.
Today I try to understand.

Yesterday you helped me cope.
Today my life is filled with hope.

Yesterday you gave me grace.
Today I bow before your face.

Yesterday you healed my sorrow.
Today I trust you for tomorrow.

Yesterday you died for me.
Today I live in victory.

Apple Cinnamon Bread

And my God will meet all your needs according to his glorious riches in Christ Jesus.

Philippians 4:19

It was my first weekend alone since we had moved to Florida. Bob had to fly back to Michigan to take care of some business matters; I cried all the way home from the airport and now sat on the sofa watching cartoons as Robby and Scott played at my feet. Though I loved them dearly, a baby and a preschooler cannot provide the emotional support a sobbing mother needs. The condo we were renting was part of a large complex where most people kept to themselves. There was no one I could call or visit, and I was desperately lonely.

I began to get angry at myself for indulging in self-pity and decided that staying inside on a gorgeous summer day was only adding to my misery. "We're going for a walk!" I announced.

With Robby on his Big Wheel and Scott in his stroller, we traveled through the web of cul-de-sacs in our complex. It felt good to be out in the warm sunshine, but seeing busy families coming and going reminded me of my loneliness. My boys soon began to sweat from the summer heat, and I decided it would be best to bring them inside.

As I turned the corner to enter our cul-de-sac, I was surprised to see a large moving van only two doors down from our condo. I tried to observe the situation as I helped Robby park his Big Wheel and lifted Scott out of his stroller. There were several people going in and out, carrying boxes, bags, and furniture.

I continued to watch through my kitchen window while my boys enjoyed playing in the cooler indoor temperature. It looked to me as though a family was moving in. There were two teen-agers, a young girl, and a middle-aged couple. *Real people!* I thought to myself as I began to get excited about the possibility of talking to someone. I wanted to run over there immediately but didn't want to get in the way.

I decided to bake a loaf of apple cinnamon bread for them. I smiled and sang cheerfully as I measured the dry ingredients, peeled the apples, and beat the eggs. My kitchen was soon en-gulfed in the delicious aroma of cinnamon as the bread began to bake and rise. When it was finally baked, cooled, sliced, and but-tered, I propped Scott on my hip, put the bread on a plate, and brought it to the neighbors with Robby following along.

"I thought you might enjoy a snack," I announced as I ap-proached the exhausted family.

"We sure would!" exclaimed the mother, wiping beads of sweat from her forehead. "How thoughtful of you!"

I chatted with the family as they stopped to take a break.

"I'm Mary Leigh," the mother informed me. "This is Sally, David, Patty, and my husband, Bill."

"What adorable children," said Sally. "I love to baby-sit, and since you're the only family I know, I hope you'll call me."

We exchanged phone numbers, and I told the kids they were welcome anytime.

In the days and weeks that followed, a friendship grew be-tween our two families. Ten-year-old Patty often came over to play with my boys; Sally turned out to be a responsible baby-sit-ter; and Mary Leigh and I went to Bible study together. I truly believe that God placed this wonderful family in our cul-de-sac because he knew they were exactly what I needed.

During our ten-month stay in Florida, I drove Bob to the airport several more times. But I didn't cry after dropping him off. Sally and Patty rode along, and we stopped at the mall on the way home.

A Glimpse of Heaven

You are all sons of God through faith in Christ Jesus.

Galatians 3:26

A child is born. He is beautiful and loved. For several years he is in a protected environment where he is safe, secure, and the center of his universe. He instinctively knows that his parents love and accept him unconditionally and that he is important to everyone. All too soon, however, the young child will notice that Jason is bigger and Tony is smarter than he is. His self-esteem is attacked, and he begins to wonder how he measures up to the superficial standards that the world has somehow managed to put into place.

At an early age, we begin to formulate our self-concept by comparing ourselves to others. As long as there are human beings on this earth, personal inequalities will exist and people will notice. There will always be those who are smarter, richer, more talented, or more beautiful than others. And, all too often, a person's worth is determined by his or her gender, intelligence, appearance, or bank account.

In Galatians 3:28, Paul states that "there is neither Jew nor Greek, there is neither slave nor free man, there is neither male nor female; for we are all one in Christ Jesus" (NASB).

Did someone say "equal"? It's a wonderful biblical principle but a difficult, if not impossible, standard by which to live—even in church!

I once had the opportunity, however, to unexpectedly experience a few moments of human equality in a small church on an Easter Sunday morning while vacationing in the Baja Peninsula. As I looked around the crowded auditorium, I noticed people of every size, shape, and color representing a variety of socioeconomic groups. In front of me was an elderly gentleman in torn, faded blue jeans, whose tanned, weathered skin told tales of hard labor. Behind me sat a young family donning the latest in designer fashions. Some women were accessorized with diamond earrings, while others wore toothless smiles. There were men in crisp, white dress shirts and men in sleeveless tees. But the beauty of this gathering was that in spite of their obvious differences, no one seemed to care. Everyone had come to worship and praise a risen Savior.

For ninety-plus minutes we sang songs of victory, meditated on God's Word, and were challenged by a faithful servant of God who shared his spiritual knowledge with eager listeners. A brief time of fellowship followed the service; then everyone scattered in different directions down the dry, dusty road. As I headed back to my motel room, I reflected on what I had just experienced. I wished that somehow the attitudes that were present in that Easter morning service could spread rapidly and contagiously throughout the whole world. Wouldn't it be wonderful if this was the norm rather than the exception? Though no one knows exactly what heaven is going to be like, I was quite sure I got a glimpse of it that morning.

Backyard Bible School

Jesus said, "Let the little children come to me, and do not hinder them, for the kingdom of heaven belongs to such as these."

Matthew 19:14

When I told five-year-old Robby that we would be out of town the week of Vacation Bible School, he was terribly disappointed.

"Maybe you can go to one at another church," I suggested.

"I won't know anyone," he argued successfully.

Then I had an idea.

"Let's have our own Bible school right here—with all your neighborhood friends. We can have it on a week when we are not on vacation."

He thought it was a good plan.

A few days later, with Scott in the stroller and Robby on his Big Wheel, we traveled up and down the sidewalks delivering the handmade invitations to our neighbors' mailboxes.

When our Bible school week finally arrived, I was pleasantly surprised: Over a dozen kids showed up on the first day. Their mothers were so grateful for a few hours of peace and quiet in their empty homes that they encouraged the children to attend the remainder of the week.

We colored pictures of Jesus, sang happy praises, and played duck-duck-goose in the grass. But most importantly, I had the opportunity to tell these children about the love of Jesus and the good news of salvation.

For the next seven summers, neighborhood children came to our backyard for Bible school. Some of the families even planned their vacations around our designated week. As the children grew, however, so did the numbers. I eventually delegated some of the responsibilities to the older children and accepted offers from two neighborhood moms who were willing to help.

Being known as "The Bible School Mom" was something that gave me great joy. My greatest joy, however, was seeing several of the children accept Jesus and become members of the kingdom of heaven.

Many of the children who listened to the Bible stories in our backyard are now married and are starting families of their own. It is my hope and prayer that they will someday have a backyard full of neighborhood children coloring pictures of Jesus, singing happy praises, and playing duck-duck-goose in the grass.

The LORD is my strength and my shield; my heart trusts in him, and I am helped.

Psalm 28:7a

I tried everything I could to comfort my two-month-old daughter, Teri, who was unusually fussy one day. I could sense something was bothering her, but I couldn't figure out what it was. I held her, rocked her, and nursed her, but nothing seemed to help. When she finally had a big dirty diaper, I figured that was the cause of the problem. She probably had some cramps, and now that "things" had passed, I was sure she would be fine.

I marveled at her soft, tiny body as I opened the messy diaper and reached for a fresh one to wrap around her bottom. "Oh, yuck!" I exclaimed when she stuck her dainty foot in the center of its contents.

As I proceeded to clean her foot, I noticed that there was something wrong with three of her toes. They were red, swollen, and bleeding, and looked as though they were cut. I immediately phoned the doctor's office to let them know I was on my way.

Upon examining my baby, the doctor determined that some fibers from her sleeper had wrapped around her toes, cutting off the circulation as well as cutting through the skin. She cried helplessly as he made repeated attempts to remove the fibers from her delicate toes. As I held her down on the table, her eyes penetrated my soul. I felt like I was betraying her by allowing this painful procedure to occur. I wanted to somehow explain that this was for her own good and that I was helping her, not hurting her.

It took the doctor more than one agonizing hour to dig the fibers from her toes. When he finally completed the procedure, the doctor and I were both emotionally exhausted and I was close to tears. "She will be fine," the doctor exclaimed with a sigh of relief as he wiped drops of sweat from his brow.

Before leaving the office, I decided to hold my daughter in my arms and nurse her in an effort to restore her faith in me. As I finally drove home, with my baby resting peacefully in her car seat, I thought about what had just occurred. This incident gave me a deeper understanding of my relationship with God. Because he loves me as his child, he may allow me to go through a painful experience for reasons I don't understand.

Just as it grieved my heart to watch my daughter suffer, it must also grieve our heavenly Father to watch his children suffer. But God is a God that can be trusted. He knows and wants what's best for us, just as a mother knows and wants what's best for her child.

If my daughter hadn't stuck her foot in the messy diaper, I don't know when I would have noticed her problem. That night, as I said my bedtime prayers, I thanked God for helping me through my difficult day, for the doctor who patiently cared for my baby, and for a big dirty diaper.

Ten Tiny Fingers

Ten tiny fingers and ten tiny toes,
    sparkling eyes and a button nose.
Too precious for words,
    so soft and so sweet,
I powder your tummy
    and tickle your feet.

For nine long months
    you tossed and you turned
    inside my body.
I desperately yearned
    to see you, to love you,
    to hold you so near—
    my bundle of warmth,
    so tender and dear.

My baby, my child—
    a miracle through me.
No greater wonder on earth
    could there be.
God is so great
    and God is so good,
    to give me the blessing
    of motherhood.

My Rocking Chair

I rocked my precious babies
In my cozy rocking chair.
I held them closely to my chest
And gently stroked their hair.

I shared the chair with Mother Goose
And bedtime lullabies.
My rocking chair was always there
For weepy, sleepy eyes.

It rocked a frightened child
Through a rumbling thunderstorm.
And when my baby had the flu
It helped me keep her warm.

It calmed a restless child
For an afternoon of rest.
And when I cuddled more than one,
It always rocked the best.

The chair sits in the corner now
So quiet and alone.
Our rocking days are in the past,
My children all have grown.

But sometimes when I'm in the mood,
I sit and rock a while.
Remembering those rocking days
Always brings a smile.

Fingerprints

There are fingerprints on the table,
There are fingerprints on the chair.
Doorknobs, walls, and bathroom sink—
There are fingerprints everywhere.

I wipe them off the windows,
I wipe them off the mirror.
No matter how I wipe and clean
They always reappear.

But sticky, grimy fingerprints
Will someday go away,
As little ones grow up to find
Another place to stay.

The windows will sparkle once again,
The doorknobs and mirrors will shine,
The walls and tables will look like new,
And all the chairs will be fine.

Someday I'll reflect and remember
The days when my children were small,
And I'll wish that I had some fingerprints
On the windows, table, or wall.

That Must Be Your Grandma!

When pride comes, then comes disgrace, but with humility comes wisdom.

Proverbs 11:2

It was a warm, spring evening as I pulled into the parking lot of the small Baptist church and carried a large box of books through the wood-carved double doors. A kind gentleman lifted the heavy load from my arms and placed the box on a rectangular table covered with a bright yellow linen tablecloth.

"Are you the guest speaker?" he inquired, assuming the obvious.

"Yes, sir, I am," I answered as I began arranging my books on the table.

"Well, here's your lapel mike," he said, handing me the tiny black piece of metal with a skinny cord that ended in a small square box I was supposed to clip somewhere on my two-piece outfit.

It was the annual mother-daughter banquet, which had been preceded by months of meticulous preparations. The delectable dinner was served by willing husbands and fathers who gracefully carried silver trays on their shoulders and balanced them with the palms of their hands. A trio of curly-haired sisters in baby-blue pinafores delighted the audience with a medley of gospel favorites, and a humorous grandmother skit had us in stitches before we marched upstairs into the auditorium for the "main event."

As I attempted to entertain and inspire the audience with my stories and poems, I could sense a warm response. Following the program, I quickly slipped behind the yellow table, hoping for a few interested customers. In no time at all, I was mobbed with women and children of all ages wanting to purchase my books.

They loved me! I thought to myself as my head began to swell.

Mothers and daughters of various generations waited patiently in line as I smiled and signed the chosen books. An adorable pre-schooler with flowing auburn locks handed me a fistful of books. "Will you please sign these?" she asked politely.

"Are you sure you may have *all* of those?" I asked, wondering if she had simply picked up an entire stack.

"I told her she could have them," came a voice from behind me.

Not getting a clear glimpse of the person who uttered the words of approval, I assumed it had to be a grandmother. "That must be your grandma," I blurted out as I winked at the young girl.

"I'm her mother," the voice from behind me corrected.

For several moments I was completely speechless. By the time I thought of something to say, the mother and daughter had disappeared into the mob of females who were now making me feel somewhat claustrophobic.

How could I be so stupid! I thought to myself as I continued to sign books and force a smile. My swelling head was appropriately deflated, as was my ego.

I searched for the mother and daughter as I packed my remaining books and left the building. I wanted a chance to apologize, but the chance never came. It was a lesson well learned, and I determined that, with God's help, I would be more careful in the future.

The following week, I spoke at a similar function. After the program, a brown-eyed cutie and a friendly woman, who I assumed to be her mother, purchased a book for me to sign.

"I told her she could have whatever she wanted," the woman informed me.

Remembering my recent experience, I looked at the little girl and commented, "That must be your sister!"

A Grandma

A grandma is someone who spoils the kids,
But somehow it seems all right.
A grandma is someone who rocks a child
Through the long, dark hours of night.

A grandma has endless patience.
A grandma has wisdom, too.
When little ones are fussy,
She knows just what to do.

A grandma reads to the children
And teaches them silly songs.
She doesn't skip the pages
When the story gets too long.

A grandma prays for her grandkids
And sends them cards in the mail.
A grandma willingly empties
The messy diaper pail.

A grandma cleans up the kitchen
And sweeps the floor with a smile.
She knows when Mother is tired
And tells her to rest for a while.

A grandma always has plenty of hugs,
For grandmas are filled with love.
A grandma is one of God's blessings
Sent from heaven above.

It's Not That Easy

Her children arise and call her blessed.

Proverbs 31:28a

During my years of teaching preschool, I was often annoyed by the irresponsibility of some of the mothers. I couldn't believe it when Amy came to school in her pink ruffled skirt and white sandals on the day we were going to the apple orchard! Then there was the time we were all loaded in the vans ready to depart to the fire station for the ultimate field trip, when I noticed we didn't have Jason's permission slip. I had to make seventeen restless children wait in the vans while I frantically called his mother.

I think the worst time, however, was when we had to send Casey home with a one hundred-and-three fever! How can a mother not know that her child is sick? I knew that if and when I became a mother, I would certainly be more aware of my child's needs.

And then I became a mother and discovered it's not that easy.

"I was the only one who didn't wear church clothes," Robby informed me after returning home from school on a Wednesday afternoon. "We went to the symphony today and were supposed to dress up."

"Well, at least you were cool and comfortable in your shorts and tennis shoes," I responded in an attempt to excuse my error.

"Did you know the teacher called me at work this morning?" my husband informed me when he came home from work one evening.

"Why on earth would she call you at work?" I asked innocently.

"It seems the kids were on the bus ready to leave for the museum, and she didn't have Scott's permission slip," he explained.

"She must have lost it," I answered.

Perhaps my most humbling moment, however, happened when I was at church having lunch with the Women's Bible Study leaders. One of the church secretaries came into our room and announced loudly, "Would Crystal Bowman please go to school and pick up her daughter. She has the chicken pox."

I thought it was a little unusual to get mosquito bites in March.

Being a mother seems like a simple job to those who have never been one. "Don't you get bored?" and "What do you do all day?" are questions I've been asked by those who can't possibly relate.

Motherhood is the most challenging, demanding, exhausting occupation in our society. It's a job that requires your undivided attention twenty-four hours a day, seven days a week—with no paycheck.

So what reason would anyone have for choosing this difficult profession? Maybe because the benefits are endless, the memories are priceless, and the rewards are eternal—just to name a few.

What I Did Today

I made a snowman pancake
With a raisin for his nose.
I wiped some sticky fingers
And I bandaged injured toes.
I found some sheets and towels
And made an awesome fort.
I lengthened pairs of overalls
That somehow got too short.
I picked some dandelions
And arranged them in a bowl.
I watched a hundred busy ants
Crawl in and out of their hole.
I taught my son the alphabet
And how to tie his shoe.
I played a game of hide-and-seek,
And sang a song or two.

I read a dozen storybooks
Of bears and frogs and mice.
And when I read *The Little Train,*
I had to read it twice.
I rocked a fussy child,
And held her in my lap.
I picked up scattered toys
While my children took a nap.
I made some oatmeal cookies
And a quart of lemonade.
I watched the clouds go by
And had a picnic in the shade.
I scrubbed some tired faces,
And shampooed dirty hair.
I taught my kids a Bible verse
And said a bedtime prayer.

I didn't sign a contract,
I didn't get a raise.
I didn't have a manager
Who offered words of praise.
I only did the greatest thing
That I know how to do.
I spent the day with children,
To shape a life or two.

Average

Someone once asked Francis of Assisi how he was able to accomplish so much. He replied, "This may be why: The Lord looked down from Heaven and said, 'Where can I find the weakest, littlest man on earth?' Then He saw me and said 'I've found him. I will work through him, and he won't be proud of it. He'll see that I am only using him because of his insignificance.'"

Uncle Ben's Quote Book

would like to remove the word *average* from every dictionary. The mere sound of this word raises my ire because I have heard it too many times in reference to me.

"Your daughter is an average student," the teachers reported to my parents year after year at parent-teacher conferences.

In college I once earned a straight A on a chemistry test and was disappointed with the C+ I was given for a final grade. When I questioned the professor about my final grade, he replied in defense, "My records show that you've only earned one A. Most of your work has been average, therefore a C+ is a fair grade."

I decided to display my straight A chemistry test in a gold frame since I would probably never earn another one.

Not only was I academically average, I was also average when it came to music. "You have a nice, average voice," the choir director exclaimed as he placed me in the back row between two above-average altos.

For several years I played violin in the orchestra, where I was again labeled average, never gaining possession of the coveted first chair. One year I was second chair, which would have been impressive except for the fact that there were only two violinists in my assigned section.

When it came to sports I was average at best. I was too short for basketball, not bad at volleyball, and actually pretty good at softball—though I never hit a home run or made a double play.

And so goes the story of my average ability.

As a young woman in my mid-twenties, I was still average, but I discovered something exciting as I studied God's Word. More often than not, the people that God chose to use were average. The Bible says that Moses was slow of speech (see Exodus 4:10), yet God chose him to lead the children of Israel out of bondage in Egypt. God used Rahab, a prostitute, to hide two Israelite spies and a young shepherd boy named David to defeat a giant. Then there was Mary, a teenage girl who was chosen by God to be the mother of his Son; and we learn from the Gospels that Jesus' disciples were average men from various walks of life.

I decided that if God used average people in the past, he could still use average people today. It occurred to me that God was more interested in my *availability* than my *ability,* and that he would fully equip me for any task he assigned.

It's been more than two decades since that enlightening discovery, and I am humbled at the wonderful things God has accomplished in my life. I am living proof that God uses average people, not because of who *we* are, but because of who *he* is. Besides, when an average woman allows God to use her, she is no longer average.

Miss Mistake

I'll never be Miss Universe
Parading in a gown.
I'll never be a beauty queen
Who earns a silver crown.
But if they held a pageant
For those who make mistakes,
I'd surely be a finalist,
'Cause I've got what it takes!

I've worn my T-shirt inside out,
I've stepped in sticky gum.
I've done a lot of other things
That qualify as "dumb."
I left my groceries at the store
And saw my empty trunk.
I washed my favorite sweater,
And I'm sad to say it shrunk.

I've locked my keys inside my car
And couldn't find the spare.
I'd rather not discuss the time
I tried to bleach my hair.
I suffered from congestion
And put eye drops in my nose.
I walked along a snowy road
In shoes with open toes.

I asked my friend when she was due,
She told me that she wasn't.
I thought that ice cream made you thin.
I found out that it doesn't.
I backed into my neighbor's car
And ran into a tree.
If anyone could win this prize,
It'd certainly be me!

But as I talk and share with friends
I get a strong suspicion
That if they held this pageant,
I would have some competition.

Second Choice

In his heart a man plans his course, but the LORD determines his steps.

Proverbs 16:9

When my first children's book was published, I became active in the local schools, performing in author's assemblies, and conducting poetry workshops in the classrooms. I wanted to share my experience with the students and teachers as well as introduce them to my poems and stories. Word of mouth spread quickly and soon I was receiving calls from teachers and principals requesting visits to a variety of schools in our area.

One Monday morning in March, I received a call from a librarian at a Christian school near our home. She explained that their school was having a week-long reading celebration and wondered if I could come on Friday for a special author's visit. I told her I was available and would be happy to come.

When Friday arrived, I spent the entire school day sharing my poems and stories with groups of enthusiastic children who responded positively to my visit. As the librarian handed me my payment and thanked me for coming on short notice, she said she had something to share with me.

"We had another author who was supposed to come today," she explained. "But things didn't work out, and at the last minute we had no one. We prayed and asked God to help us find some-one else. One of our teachers thought of you, and the fact that you were available was an answer to our prayer."

Something similar occurred when I was asked to speak at a mother-daughter banquet. "I don't want you to think you're our second choice," the woman said, apologizing for her last-minute phone call, "but the speaker we scheduled had something unex-pected come up, and you would really be an answer to prayer."

And then there was the time I received a desperate plea from a dear friend of mine who is a reading specialist in a nearby school district. "I need your help!" she begged. "The author who's com-ing next week just informed us that he doesn't do programs for lower elementary. If we don't have someone for the younger kids, they will be so disappointed! I prayed that you'd be available."

I was.

There is nothing more exciting or humbling than being an answer to someone's prayer and a part of God's plan. Whenever I have the opportunity to be a substitute speaker, I am not offended that I'm their "second choice," because I would rather be "God's choice." When our well-intentioned plans go asunder, God's sovereign plans miraculously fall into place.

I have several speaking engagements on my calendar for the coming year and anticipate wonderful moments sharing my pas-sions with those who are willing to listen.

I also have some empty spaces on my calendar—just in case God has something more planned for me.

Equipped

God will equip you for every good task.
He'll give you the strength for whatever he asks.

No matter the challenge or role you must fill,
He knows what it takes to accomplish his will.

He'll give you the wisdom and courage you'll need
To serve him completely in thought, word, or deed.

You don't have to doubt, worry, or fear.
He'll never forsake you, he'll always be near.

So when you are sure that you've heard the Lord's
      voice,
Just trust and obey him, for that's the best choice.

Lori's Story

For to me, to live is Christ and to die is gain.

Philippians 1:21

Lori was a bouncy, energetic teenager with sparkling brown eyes and a contagious smile. Raised in a Christian home with godly parents, Lori possessed a spiritual maturity that set her apart from many others her age. She loved the Lord her God with all her heart, soul, and mind, and she professed her faith before her congregation at the age of sixteen.

Lori lived each day of her life in a loving relationship with her heavenly Father, seeking wisdom and guidance through prayer and meditation on his Word. She was actively involved in her youth group and went on a summer mission trip while still in high school. After graduating from high school, Lori pursued a college education in hopes of becoming an elementary school teacher. She also hoped to marry her boyfriend, who planned to become a minister. But she knew there was something more—something bigger that God had planned for her. *I know you have something special planned for me,* Lori wrote in her journal one day. *Help me to carry it out. Use me, God.*

Then one evening, when she was on a date with her boyfriend, she experienced severe abdominal pains. Her boyfriend took her to the hospital, where she was admitted for surgery. The next day, with tears in his eyes, the surgeon explained that he had removed a malignant tumor the size of a football. He said that the cancer already had a relentless grip on her body and there wasn't much they could do.

Lori didn't cry when she heard the news. She knew her God would give her the strength to fight this battle and that he would not leave her. She found much comfort in Scripture and claimed God's many promises. One of her favorite verses was Isaiah 41:10: "So do not fear, for I am with you; do not be dismayed, for I am your God. I will strengthen you and help you; I will uphold you with my righteous right hand."

Enduring aggressive chemotherapy treatments that made her very sick, Lori spent many weeks in and out of the hospital. But even though the cancer was ravaging her body, it never touched her cheerful spirit or the bright smile on her face.

Lori had a passionate desire to use her illness as a way of encouraging others, especially young people. She spoke at a convention where she boldly challenged nearly two thousand teenagers to face their future with a Christ-centered focus. "Live and die with your life anchored in the Lord Jesus Christ," she spoke with conviction. "You do not know what tomorrow will hold. Live today happily for Christ, and he will take care of your tomorrows."

Lori ended her speech with Jesus' words from 2 Corinthians 12:9, "My grace is sufficient for you, for my power is made perfect in weakness." She then added her own testimony by quoting the apostle Paul from the rest of that verse: "Most gladly therefore will I rather glory in my infirmities, that the power of Christ may rest upon me" (KJV).

With news that the cancer was growing, Lori went back to the hospital for more treatments. She shared her love for the Lord with everyone who entered her hospital room. Doctors, nurses, family, friends, and even other patients were asked the same question—"Do you know the Lord Jesus as your Savior?"

Though Lori endured much pain and suffering, she never complained and always found a reason to praise the Lord. At the age of twenty, only nine months after she learned of her cancer, Lori left her earthly home and went to be with her Lord and Savior.

Lori's testimony, however, didn't end with her death. Her story of triumph was broadcast over a Christian radio program that aired throughout the United States and Canada and even into areas of Poland. Requests from listeners poured into the station asking for cassette copies of Lori's story. "I need to send this to a friend," wrote a woman from New York. "I want to use this story with our patients," stated a listener from Wisconsin. "It was a touch of God," added a man from California whose wife had cancer.

The story of Lori's powerful testimony was also incorporated into a church school curriculum, so that her message to young people would continue to be heard.

Lori knew God had big plans for her, and because she allowed him to use her, those plans were bigger and better than she could have imagined. Many people, young and old, accepted Lori's challenge to live their lives for Jesus—and that's exactly what she wanted.

Remember That God Is Near

When you're smothered by problems and life seems unfair,
When it seems as though there is nobody there,
When you're looking for someone to listen and care,
Remember that God is near.

When friends disappoint you and go their own way,
When you'd rather not face another bad day,
When you can't even find the right words to pray,
Remember that God is near.

When you need some directions and feel like you're lost,
When your life's like a ship being tumbled and tossed,
When you wish there was someone to guide you across,
Remember that God is near.

When you're searching for hope and praying for peace,
When you're longing for trials to finally cease,
When you fervently pray for your strength to increase,
Remember that God is near.

When you lean on your faith and stop asking why,
When your smile returns and your tears become dry,
When you see God's rainbow up in the sky,
You will know that God is near.

Bon Voyage

I wish that I could take a trip
And leave my cares behind.
I'd pack my bags with hopes and dreams,
And things to ease my mind.
I'd travel to a better place
Where troubles disappear,
Where peace and comfort follow me,
And joy replaces fear.

I'd wake each morning with the sun
And have no need to worry—
Carefree, happy, safe, secure,
And never in a hurry.
I'd live my life abundantly,
And throw away my sorrow.
Embracing laughter, life, and love,
I'd welcome each tomorrow.

But as I think about this place
And wish that it could be,
The Lord says, "You will be there,
When you cast your cares on me."

Close Call

The LORD will keep you from all harm—he will watch over your life; the LORD will watch over your coming and going both now and forevermore.

Psalm 121:7–8

The personal interview on the 6:00 news was chilling. A passenger thought he was having a bad day. He missed his airplane; then he lost a dollar in the vending machine. It would be enough to make even the most patient person a little frustrated. He soon discovered, however, that he was not having a bad day after all. Shortly after take-off, the airplane that contained his empty seat plunged into the reptile-infested waters of the Everglades, killing all on board.

Though my experience was not as dramatic, I also had a "close call" with my three children. I was planning on spending the day at my mother's house, which was a forty-five minute drive from our home. As mothers of young children know, getting your children out of the house and into the car is more than half the battle. As I was backing out of the driveway, four-year-old Scott announced that he was thirsty. Although I dreaded going back into the house, I knew if I didn't get him a drink, the next forty-five minutes of my life would not be pleasant. I went into the house, poured apple juice into his sippy-cup, brought it out to the car, then once again backed out of the driveway to begin the journey.

As I approached the entrance to the expressway, a police officer pulled in front of me and prevented me from continuing in that direction. A cloud of thick, black smoke swirling into the air signaled that something terrible had happened. Seeking an alternate route, I turned on the radio and was soon informed that a tanker transporting flammable liquid had overturned and exploded, killing the driver as well as two passengers in a nearby vehicle. If I hadn't gone back into the house to get my son a drink, my vehicle could have been the one that went up in flames. It occurred to me that Scott's need for a drink could have been God's divine intervention protecting me from danger.

Many times we are frustrated by delays and interruptions in our lives. We are intent on our own agenda and annoyed by anything that stands in our way. When we remind ourselves, however, that God's agenda is the one to pursue, we can accept the unexpected as God's sovereign plan for our lives.

I guess I'll never know for sure if this incident was God's protection, but it changed my attitude toward thirsty little boys.

Invisible

"Thou art a God who sees."

Genesis 16:13b NASB

I patiently waited in line as the clerk behind the service counter helped the customers in front of me. After he listened to explanations for returned items, stamped packages to be mailed, and gave a cash refund for sour milk, it was finally my turn to be helped. Just as I was about to request two books of postage stamps, a young woman jumped in front of me and announced that she needed to send a fax. When the clerk began helping her, I promptly interrupted, "Uh, excuse me, but I was next in line."

"Oh, I'm terribly sorry, I didn't see you," apologized the clerk as the young woman stepped aside with an attitude.

Didn't *see* me? At five feet, two and a half inches tall, I know I'm not a giant, but I'm certainly not invisible.

It happened again a few days later when I was standing at the deli case in the supermarket. A busy clerk sliced and weighed twelve ounces of Swiss cheese and sixteen ounces of honey-baked ham. She packaged the items neatly in cellophane bags, then handed them to the woman next to me. As the satisfied customer wheeled her cart toward the checkout aisle, the deli clerk disappeared behind stainless steel doors leaving me drooling over trays of mesquite turkey breast and olive-pepper loaf.

I promptly pressed the *please ring bell for service* button, which magically brought the woman bounding through the double doors. "Oh, I'm sorry," she apologized, "I didn't see anyone out here."

Didn't *see* anyone? Is everyone in the world nearsighted, or am I truly invisible?

This sort of thing not only happens to me at service counters and deli cases, but I've also had people not *see* me at the post office, gas station, and clothing stores. I've wondered if, perhaps, some of these people have such rich imaginations that while they are physically working, their minds are entertaining them with trips to the Bahama Islands. Or maybe, if I'm not invisible, I somehow blend in with my surroundings like a chameleon. Maybe someday I'll have the nerve to ask.

It's comforting to know, however, that God sees me at all times. And when I want to talk to God, I don't have to wait in line at a counter, take a number, or press a service button. God is available twenty-four hours a day, seven days a week. He not only sees me, but he knows what I need even before I ask. Psalm 139:4 says, "Before a word is on my tongue you know it completely, O Lord."

I'm sure I'll have more incidences when clerks don't see me, but I know I can always count on my heavenly Father to see me, hear me, and know exactly what I need.

The Missing Ingredient

If I have the gift of prophecy and can fathom all mysteries and all knowledge, and if I have a faith that can move mountains, but have not love, I am nothing.

1 Corinthians 13:2

Sitting on my kitchen counter were four almost rotten bananas. My conscience told me what I needed to do—preheat the oven to 350 degrees and get out the flour, sugar, shortening, milk, and eggs. Thumbing through my dilapidated recipe box, I found my favorite banana bread recipe on a stained index card. As I measured, poured, beat, and blended the various ingredients, I envisioned the delighted expressions on my family members' faces when I offered them warm, buttered slices of homemade banana bread.

I glanced at the recipe card one last time before carefully transferring the batter from the mixing bowl to the greased bread pans waiting to be filled. Into the oven went the pans as I set the timer to one hour and ten minutes. By the time I finished washing the bowl, spoons, and spatula, a tantalizing aroma permeated the kitchen, making me feel like "Homemaker of the Year." I was pleased with my successful attempt to save the bananas and could hardly wait for the words of praise I would soon be receiving for my dedicated efforts.

Shortly before the timer was about to buzz, I turned on the oven light to take a quick peek at the rising loaves of bread. To my astonishment, the loaves were not rising. The batter had transformed into two firm mounds of paste. I reread the recipe card and realized I had left out one simple ingredient—baking soda!

As I tearfully scooped two large clumps of banana bread failure down the garbage disposal, I realized that I had not only wasted the four bananas but also the flour, sugar, shortening, milk, and eggs! It amazed me that one tiny teaspoon of baking soda could have made the difference between total disaster and taste bud bliss.

In 1 Corinthians 13, the Bible talks about a necessary ingredient—not for banana bread but for everyday living. It says that if we lack love, we are nothing. We can be gifted, knowledgeable speakers, have faith to move mountains, and give all we have to the poor, but if we do not have love, our talents, efforts, and deeds are useless. Love is the key ingredient to a happy, productive, meaningful life. Without love, everything we do is in vain.

The love discussed in 1 Corinthians 13 is unconditional love—the kind of love that God has for his people. He loves and accepts us in spite of our shortcomings and failures. He loves us even when we disappoint him or disobey his Word. Unconditional love is the hardest kind of love to show others, but it's the kind of love that is necessary in order for our lives to be purposeful and pleasing to God.

In everything we do, whether it is at the office, in the home, or in our church or community, we are required by God to do it in love. And when it comes to making banana bread, you can include the love, but don't forget the baking soda!

The Greatest Is Love

Perfect love is hard to find,
For love is patient, gentle, and kind.
Love is humble rather than proud.
Love is not rude, angry, or loud.
Love does not envy.
Love never fails.
Love rejoices when truth prevails.

Love is unselfish, it doesn't do wrong.
Love will endure
And always be strong.
Love always hopes,
It always believes.
Love turns from sin,
It never deceives.

Love, hope, and faith
Are gifts from above.
These three will remain,
But the greatest is love.

Based on 1 Corinthians 13

Sometimes

I like to make meals for my family,
But sometimes I burn the food.
I like to be perky and cheerful,
But sometimes that's not my mood.

I like my house to be tidy and clean,
But sometimes it is a mess.
I like to be smart and know all the facts,
But sometimes I have to guess.

I like my kids to be wise and mature,
But sometimes they make mistakes.
I like to be able to handle it all,
But sometimes I lack what it takes.

I like to be strong and confident,
But sometimes I'm not that way.
When things aren't how I like them to be,
Sometimes it's really okay.

Folding Towels

He enjoys much who is thankful for little.

Uncle Ben's Quote Book

I have a cousin who has spent most of her adult life in foster care or nursing homes. Every time I visit her, I go with the intent of brightening her day. I am the one, however, who is repeatedly blessed by our time together. Marion's confinement to a wheelchair, combined with her humble surroundings, would make most people pity her seemingly empty life. But anyone who shares a few moments with her will soon discover that her life is far from empty.

The secret to Marion's happy, fulfilling life is that she embraces with joy the blessings God has given her, rather than dwelling on what she lacks. She has learned to appreciate the little things in life that most people take for granted. Marion is thankful for the window in her tiny room that allows her to enjoy the beauties of God's creation. "I love watching the birds find their food and the shapely clouds sweep through the sky," she expresses joyfully.

Marion is also thankful for the radio in her room that provides hours of spiritual enrichment and keeps her informed on current events. She usually fills me in on the latest happenings to which I am totally ignorant.

Though Marion is not able to attend the church to which she belongs, the weekly bulletin rests on her bedside nightstand. Every day, as Marion reads and rereads its contents, she prays for the names and events that are listed. "I don't know all the people, and I can't participate in the activities, but I can pray for them," she says with a sense of responsibility.

During one of our visits, Marion informed me with childlike enthusiasm that she had been given a job.

"I get to fold the towels when they are fresh and dry!" she stated proudly.

She went on to explain that folding the towels not only makes her feel useful but also gives her an opportunity to honor God by doing her best.

Marion's example of a Christ-centered, thankful life has convicted me many times over. When I'm tempted to complain about making beds, ironing dress shirts, or packing school lunches, I remind myself that these mundane tasks should be regarded as privileges rather than chores. Maintaining a positive focus and an attitude of thankfulness is a daily challenge. But every once in a while, when I have a load of fresh, dry towels to fold, I try to do it with a smile.

Spring Cleaning

It's time to clean the closets
And scrub the kitchen floors.
It's time to wash the windows
And open up the doors.

Winter days are passing,
It's time to welcome spring.
The sun caresses us with warmth,
And newborn robins sing.

But as you do your cleaning,
Please take a look inside.
Perhaps you need to scrub away
Some selfishness or pride.

Do cobwebs of self-pity
Clutter up your mind,
Making thoughts of thankfulness
So difficult to find?

Do bitterness and gossip
Make your life a mess,
Keeping you from serving God
And doing what is best?

Then seek the Lord's forgiveness
And let the Spirit in,
For he alone can give you hope
And cleanse your life from sin.

He can take your filthy rags
And make them just like new,
So that your life will honor him
In everything you do.

Then you'll know the peace and joy
That life in Christ will bring.
The testimony from your lips
Will be as fresh as spring.

House and Home

A house is made of mortar and brick,
Windowpanes and doors.
A house is made of sturdy walls,
Painted ceilings and floors.

A house is a place that can keep you safe
Whether it's large or small,
But through the years of wind and rain
A house can crumble and fall.

A home is made of family and friends
Who laugh and play and share.
A home is made of people who give,
Who help each other and care.

A home is a place for comfort and hope
Where broken hearts are restored.
A home is a place for praise and prayer,
And blessing from the Lord.

A home is a place that can keep you safe
Whether it's large or small,
And through the years of trials and pain
A home can endure it all.

When Guests Come to Stay

When guests come to stay
We are always polite.
We try not to grumble,
Holler, or fight.

When guests come to stay
We are patient and kind,
Respectful and thoughtful,
Poised and refined.

When guests come to stay
We plan and prepare.
We offer our best
To show that we care.

But doesn't your family
Deserve what is best?
Don't they mean more
Than a visit from guests?

Perhaps we should live
And behave every day,
The way that we do
When guests come to stay.

Whose Day Is Tuesday?

Never speak loudly to one another unless the house is on fire.

Uncle Ben's Quote Book

*I*t's not fair! You always get to sit in the front!" scream one sibling to another.

Mention the words "sibling rivalry" to any mother, and watch her emotion meter tick! The fact that it occurs in almost every family with more than one child is neither comforting nor reassuring. Sibling rivalry is unpleasant, frustrating, and emotionally exhausting.

So what's the answer besides duct-taping their mouths? Even though it's important to teach children that life is not *always* fair, we were able to establish a sense of fairness in our home by assigning each of our three children two days per week to be "their" days. On "their" day, that child could sit in the front seat of the car, choose the television programs, use the Mickey Mouse cup, and decide whether we would play Candy Land, Sorry, or Chutes and Ladders.

Along with being the privileged child, however, came responsibilities. On "their" day, they also had to help with dishes, lead prayer time at the table, and be the first one in the tub.

We used this system for over a decade, and it worked beautifully. Throughout the day, as minor squabbles occurred, I simply had to say, "Whose day is it?" and the problem would soon be solved. Though it did not completely eliminate sibling rivalry, I believe it gave our children a realistic sense of fairness and cooperation in our home. They were usually cooperative when it wasn't their day, because they knew their day was coming soon.

Sibling rivalry is nothing new. The first book of the Bible records several unpleasant encounters between family members. The first murder occurs in Genesis 4, when Cain kills his brother Abel out of jealousy. Later on, we read the story of Joseph and his jealous brothers. Perhaps they wouldn't have hated him if they each had "their" day to wear the colorful coat. Then there were Jacob and Esau, whose relationship was one of deceit rather than brotherly love.

It's painful for mothers to see their children argue and fight, because we love each one so dearly. If your children are the appropriate age for the "days of the week" system, try using it for a while to see if it makes a difference in your home.

And by the way—*my* day is Sunday!

Breakfast on the Sidewalk

"Then the righteous will answer him, 'Lord, when did we see you hungry and feed you, or thirsty and give you something to drink? When did we see you a stranger and invite you in, or needing clothes and clothe you? When did we see you sick or in prison and go to visit you?'

"The King will reply, 'I tell you the truth, whatever you did for one of the least of these brothers of mine, you did for me.'"

Matthew 25:37–40

One Labor Day weekend, Bob and I decided to whisk our kids away to Chicago for one last mini-vacation before the demands of elementary and middle school and extracurricular activities dictated our schedules. Our children were fascinated with the exhibits, movies, and hands-on activities at the Museum of Science and Industry. They patiently tolerated the long lines and inquisitive audience as we attempted to get a glimpse of the Monet exhibit at the Art Institute. They were in more comfortable territory at Nike Town and enjoyed a juicy chicken sandwich at Michael Jordan's restaurant. They absorbed the breathtaking view of the city from the peak of the Sears Tower and even dressed up for a formal evening dinner. But it was our Monday morning breakfast that they will never forget.

We decided to grab a quick breakfast at a fast-food restaurant across from our hotel. As we approached the entrance, a shabbily dressed man sitting on the sidewalk asked us for money. Bob shook his head while we quickly and silently walked past.

"Why didn't you give him any money?" Teri inquired once we were inside.

"Do you remember that time in Kentucky," Bob explained, "when we gave that guy some money and then we saw him go into a bar?"

"Oh, yeah," she recalled. "He probably used it for beer."

"I have a better idea," Bob continued, "but let's eat our breakfast first."

My kids raised their eyebrows and shrugged their shoulders, wondering what their dad had in mind. When we finished eating, Bob went back to the counter and ordered a breakfast to go.

"Give this to the man on the sidewalk," my husband instructed as he handed the bag to Teri.

Her big brothers protectively escorted her as she delivered the breakfast to the man, who was still sitting in the same spot.

"Here's some breakfast," Teri said, offering him the bag.

"God bless you, child," he replied with a smile as he eagerly received the bagged breakfast.

As we walked back to the hotel to get our luggage for our return trip home, Teri exclaimed, "That was the best part of our whole vacation!"

There are needy people in every community. Donating clothing or giving financially to local missions and world relief organizations can help many who are less fortunate. And if you ever have the opportunity to respond spontaneously to someone with an immediate need, do it. It will make your day!

Love One Another

"You must love one another
As I have loved you."
This is what Christ Jesus
Commands us all to do.
Well, I can love my husband,
My mother and my dad.
And I can love my children—
Even when they're bad!

I can love my Christian friends
And help them when they're sick.
I can give a holy hug
To those within my clique.
But Lord, I have this neighbor,
She's crabby and she's mean.
And she has the weirdest husband
That you have ever seen.

And people that are dirty
Really turn me off.
I never sit by anyone
Who has a hacking cough.
I never talk to strangers,
I just don't think I should.
Especially when I know they're from
Another neighborhood.

People who are different
Should just be left alone.
I know you don't expect me
To invite them in my home.
Lord, you know I'm busy,
And love takes so much time.
Surely all those other folks
Will get along just fine.

But as I search the Scriptures,
The truth I clearly see,
The Lord says, "If you don't love them,
You really don't love me."

Why Am I Surprised?

Why am I surprised
when God answers prayer?
Do I think he doesn't listen?
Do I wonder if he's there?

I pray for peace and very soon
he calms my doubts and fears.
I ask God for direction
and he guides me through the years.

I ask the Lord to use me
and give me strength each day.
So why am I surprised
when these blessings come my way?

The Lord is always willing
to listen to my plea,
and so I should expect him
to hear and answer me.

He wants me to confide in him,
to give him every care.
And so I shouldn't be surprised
when God answers prayer.

A Joyful Lunch

You have made known to me the path of life; you will fill me with joy in your presence, with eternal pleasures at your right hand.

Psalm 16:11

Staying in touch with some of my high school friends has been a special blessing in my life. There are about ten of us who try to get together almost every year. We talk about our husbands, kids, and extended families but spend most of our time laughing hysterically as we reminisce about the good ol' days.

One particular day they were coming to my house for lunch. With childlike anticipation, I arranged the china place settings on my dining room table, knowing we'd be glued to the chairs until someone realized she should have left hours earlier. As the doorbell rang, I greeted my friends with hugs and relieved them of the salads and muffins they brought.

"Is Sharon coming?" asked Karen as we found our places around the table.

"She should be here soon," I informed her. "They're camping up north about an hour away, but she said she wouldn't miss this for anything."

"I heard she's doing really well," Judy commented positively. "It's already been three months since her mastectomy."

"It will be great to see her," I replied.

The doorbell rang again, and this time it was Sharon.

"You look good, Sharon," I said sincerely as I embraced her and let her in.

Sharon quickly joined us at the table and began telling us the whole story, from the minute she discovered the lump to her current trips to the hospital for chemotherapy.

"I feel great!" Sharon reassured us. "Except for the horrible hot flashes. But most of all, I've learned to take life one day at a time and trust the Lord for everything."

Later that afternoon, as I was loading my china into the dishwasher, I kept thinking about Sharon. She seemed so happy in spite of everything. Her disease didn't dampen her spirit, dim her bright smile, or destroy the positive attitude she always seems to have.

Sharon has joy! I thought to myself. *This is what we've been talking about in Bible study.* I felt as though I had just gained a deeper insight into the definition of joy: *True joy is being happy in spite of your circumstances, not because of them.*

God doesn't promise that we'll never have problems, but he does promise to help us deal with them. And knowing that God can help us climb our biggest mountain or lift us out of our deepest valley, we can still have joy in the midst of our trials. In his presence there is fullness of joy.

Joy

It's easy to be happy
When everything is fine.
We can wear a friendly smile,
And be pleasant all the time.

When life is free of trials,
We can lift our hands and pray.
We can praise the Lord for blessings
And be thankful for each day.

But can we find true happiness
Through all the storms of life?
Can we wear a friendly smile
In the midst of pain and strife?

Can we thank the Lord for blessings
When our life is filled with sorrow?
Can we cling to all his promises
And look beyond tomorrow?

For when we turn to Jesus
With our problems and our pain,
When we thank him for his goodness
Through the sunshine and the rain,

When we wear a friendly smile
Even though we have a need,
When we trust him for tomorrow,
We will find true joy, indeed.

Two Best Friends

Two best friends like to pretend,
they dress their teddy bears,
who quietly sit in buttoned coats,
for Sunday school on the stairs.

Two best friends like to ride bikes
and jump rope after class.
They share a stick of bubble gum
and do cartwheels in the grass.

Two best friends are inseparable.
They stay up on Friday night,
sharing secrets and pizza with cheese
till Mother turns out the light.

Two best friends are growing up,
they trade in their dolls and toys
for panty hose and lipstick,
and magazines and boys.

Two best friends talk on the phone
discussing what they will wear
their very first day of high school,
and what should they do with their hair?

Two best friends excited and scared
going out on a double date,
trying on clothes and watching the clock,
hoping they won't be late.

Two best friends walk down the aisle
on their graduation day.

They promise they'll always stay in touch
as each goes her separate way.

Two best friends like to send notes
and visit whenever they can,
sharing their latest hopes and dreams
and talk about wedding plans.

Two best friends longing for moments
to spend some time with each other,
to share their tales of labor pains
and the joys of being a mother.

Two best friends with tears in their eyes
bring their children to school.
"They're growing up much too fast!
I hope the kids won't be cruel."

Two best friends meet for lunch,
their children are leaving home.
Yesterday they were babies,
and now they are out on their own.

Two best friends talking together
as proud as they can be,
showing pictures of grandkids
and sharing a pot of tea.

Two best friends are growing old.
They talk about days in the past,
wondering how it is possible
that life goes by so fast.

Two best friends are thankful to God
as life finally comes to an end,
for the blessings and joys, laughter and tears,
that were shared with a very best friend.

Eight Quarters

Not what we get, but what we give, measures the worth of the life we live.

Uncle Ben's Quote Book

I had just spent an eight-hour day at a local women's conference and was eager to get home. One of my pet peeves is having to wait in line in order to exit a parking ramp. When an event is over, so is my patience. The line moved at a snail's pace, but finally I reached the exit booth.

"That will be eight dollars, please," the parking attendant informed me.

I handed him a ten-dollar bill and was inwardly annoyed with the two dollars' worth of quarters he handed me in return.

"Sorry, ma'am," he apologized. "I'm all out of ones."

Since I had just spoken on the importance of having a positive attitude, I assured him that it was no problem and thanked him for his help. I stuffed the eight quarters in my already bulging coin purse and planned on transferring them to my loose change cup in the kitchen once I arrived home. Being greeted with hungry appetites, however, I quickly made dinner and completely forgot about the quarters.

Two days later, I sat behind a small wooden table at a bookstore, hoping for a few interested customers who would be delighted with an autographed copy of one of my books. A book signing may seem to some like a glamorous event, but in reality, it is usually quite humbling. Many people walk by and stare, wondering why you're just sitting there doing nothing. Some think I'm a store employee and ask where they can find various titles from the best-sellers' list, none of which happen to be mine. Others ask me the time, directions to the food court, or if they may please use the rest room. One time I agreed to watch a mother's three young children while she went to get her purse, which she had left on the front seat of her car.

This particular afternoon, I actually had a few people purchase some of my books and ask me to sign them. After three long hours, as I started packing up my things, a sweet young woman appeared out of nowhere and asked if she could see some of my books. She informed me that she had a disability that made reading a challenge for her. She added that she had been taking some classes and that her reading skills were gradually improving.

"I can read this one," she announced proudly as she picked up one of my chapter books. "How much is it?"

"The paperback is only five dollars," I replied enthusiastically.

As she dug into her purse, the excitement on her face was quickly replaced with a look of disappointment.

"I only have three dollars and enough change to cover the tax," she explained. "Do you think they'll hold it for me for a few days?"

All at once my mind flashed back to the eight quarters in my coin purse.

"Hey, guess what?" I told her. "I got a bunch of quarters the other day that I want to get rid of."

Without waiting for her to answer, I took out the quarters and placed them in her hand.

"It's just the right amount," she exclaimed happily as she added up the money.

"Will you please sign the book and also put my name in it?"

"It would be my pleasure," I replied.

I wrote the following inscription: "To my friend, Gina, from Crystal Bowman," dated it, and handed her the book.

"You must be a Christian," she stated boldly.

"Yes, I am," I said. "And how about you?"

"Oh, definitely!" she answered.

"Well then," I added, "we're not only friends, but we're also sisters in Christ."

While Gina walked toward the cash register, I finished packing up my belongings. As far as book signings go, my afternoon wasn't all that impressive. But I certainly made a worthwhile investment with my two dollars' worth of quarters.

A Woman Who Is Wise

A woman who is wise is patient and kind.
She speaks the truth in love when words are hard to find.
She finds the good in others and offers words of praise.
Many are encouraged by her understanding ways.

She listens very carefully, with confidence she speaks.
Finding truth and knowledge is something that she seeks.
She knows her gifts and talents, her limitations too.
She wisely makes commitments for the things she wants
   to do.

She plans for the future but lives for today.
She labors with endurance, yet takes the time to play.
She cares for her body with exercise and rest.
She is modern but she's modest when she tries to look
   her best.

And whether she's a mother, a sister, or a wife,
Her wisdom comes from God, for she's given him her life.
She often studies Scripture, she goes to God in prayer.
She finds him as a faithful friend, the one who's always there.

Her faith in God is steadfast, though trials come her way.
She trusts him for tomorrow, and leans on him today.
She doesn't long for riches, or things she can't afford.
She knows she'll be rewarded for her service to the Lord.

She reaches out to those in need, she's quick to lend a hand.
Many share their problems, for she seems to understand.
She doesn't care for gossip or believe in foolish lies.
For she's a godly woman, she's a woman who is wise.

A Time to Praise

Praise the LORD. Praise God in his sanctuary; praise him in his mighty heavens. Praise him for his acts of power; praise him for his surpassing greatness. Let everything that has breath praise the LORD. Praise the LORD.

Psalm 150:1, 2, 6

It's easy to go to God in prayer when we have a need: *Lord, help me get this job. Heal my mother's cancer. Give my sister a child.* But even though God wants us to come to him with our problems and needs, far too often our needs dominate our prayers. God also desires and deserves our praise. It's important to have balance in our prayer life, to spend as much time praising as we do asking.

In our women's Bible study, I learned the following acrostic:

Adoration. Praise God for his attributes, his greatness, and his mighty deeds.

Confession. Confess your sins and ask God's forgiveness.

Thanksgiving. Thank God for all the good things he's given you.

Supplication. Bring your needs before God and trust him to fulfill them.

Following this pattern of prayer helps me to recognize God's greatness and goodness, rather than focusing only on my needs. I have also found that reading the Psalms results in an attitude of praise. And one day, just for fun, I decided to write my own psalm of praise.

A Psalm of Praise

Give praise to God and bless his name,
For he alone is good.
He made the sun, the moon, and stars,
The rivers, lakes, and wood.

He made the birds and flowers,
The mountains capped with snow.
The universe is in his hand,
He will not let it go.

He knows all things, he sees all things,
He hears a child's prayer.
Every creature he has made
Is always in his care.

When we call upon his name,
He listens to our plea.
Walking in his perfect will
Is where we ought to be.

Give praise to God and bless his name.
Give thanks to God above.
Praise him for his greatness,
His mercy and his love.

A Rich Example

"Do not store up for yourselves treasures on earth, where moth and rust destroy, and where thieves break in and steal. But store up for yourselves treasures in heaven, where moth and rust do not destroy, and where thieves do not break in and steal. For where your treasure is, there your heart will be also. . . . But seek first his kingdom and his righteousness, and all these things will be given to you as well."

Matthew 6:19–21, 33

I was listening to a humorous lecturer on PBS. "My parents were poor," he confessed, "but I didn't know it."

My childhood experience was the opposite. My parents were rich, but I didn't know it. We weren't Donald Trump rich, but my father owned a construction company, and, with only an eighth-grade education, was a successful businessman. I knew that my father had a good job and that he could adequately provide for a few "wants" as well as our needs, but I never thought of our family as being rich. With a family of six, we grew up in a modest three-bedroom ranch with a two-stall garage. With the exception of a small summer cottage and a boat, we didn't own much more than anyone else in the neighborhood.

My parents were very generous and were always hard workers. They lived by the "early to bed, early to rise" proverb and devoted their lives to caring for our family and reaching out to those in our church and community who had a need. My mother gave our clothes away as soon as we outgrew them and was constantly in the kitchen making casseroles or baked goods for church and school activities. My father often donated his time and skills to help a number of causes, and I remember a time when he sent money to his younger brother in California so that his family could join us in Michigan for a summer reunion. It seemed like everything we owned was available to anyone who needed it. People frequently borrowed my father's trucks, and almost everyone we knew visited our cottage at one time or another.

My father also had a burden for the lost and a passion for evangelism. When he discovered a poverty-stricken slum a few miles away from our cottage, he bought some property, built a chapel, found a preacher, and began a ministry. He canvassed the dirt roads on foot, going house to house, inviting the people to come to church. Recognizing their physical needs as well as their spiritual needs, he saw to it that food and clothing were available to those who came to the worship service. The ministry flourished for years, and because of my father's vision, several of these forgotten people will have a mansion in glory.

My parents are still living in their modest three-bedroom ranch and still rise early to make the most of their day. They have enough financial security to see them through retirement, but they have much more waiting for them in heaven where they have stored up most of their treasures. I know that when the Lord finally calls them home, he will say to each of them, "Well done, thou good and faithful servant."

> Treasures that we store on earth
> Will fade away and lose their worth.
> But when we live for Jesus Christ,
> Our treasures have a lasting price.

My Mother and I

My mother kneaded homemade bread.
I buy mine at the store.
My mother hung the laundry out.
I close my dryer door.
My mother scrubbed the vegetables
She grew and picked herself.
But mine come in a plastic bag
Or a can from off the shelf.

My mother got her hair done
Every week at a salon.
But all I need to do
Is turn my curling iron on.
My mother wore a housedress
And her stockings every day.
I wear my jeans and tennis shoes
As I go on my way.

But though our times keep changing
And the styles come and go,
The life my mother lived
Is now the life I've come to know.

My mother read her Bible
And she prayed to God each day.
Like her, I also read God's Word
And often pause to pray.
My mother helped the neighbors,
And cared for those in need.
I know I'm walking in her shoes
When I do thoughtful deeds.

My mother's faithful service
To her friends and family,
Provided an example
Of the way things ought to be.
And even though old-fashioned ways
To me seem rather strange,
The things that really matter
Are the things that never change.

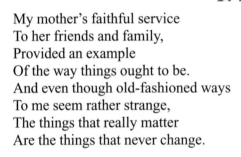

Almost Migraine

I always thank my God as I remember you in my prayers.

Philemon 4

I always enjoy the opportunity to be involved in programs that are designed to encourage and inspire mothers as they face the daily challenges of raising their children. It's not that I am an expert on raising kids, it's just that I've "been there and done it," and that allows me to share from experience.

At one particular weekend conference, I had a twofold purpose. I was there to promote some of my children's books for a publishing company as well as to speak to a group of mothers who were interested in writing for children.

Friday's schedule was hectic, to say the least. Traveling to an unfamiliar town, setting up an exhibition booth, attending an evening social function, and getting to bed too late took a toll on my body. Saturday morning began early with a raisin bagel and a taxi ride to the convention center. The first item on my agenda was a book signing, immediately followed by the session with aspiring writers.

Halfway into my book signing, as I smiled and chatted with young mothers who seemed to have far more energy than I did, I noticed the all too familiar strobe light on the right side of my peripheral vision. This signal from my brain warned me that a full-blown migraine was on its way and would soon monopolize my body. But there was nothing I could do. I couldn't lie down, take a break, or even take an aspirin. I was actually too busy to think about it and tried my best to ignore it.

As I continued talking to mothers and signing books for their precious little ones, I suddenly realized that the aura no longer existed. For some unknown reason, the aura disappeared and the migraine never showed up.

I finished the book signing, grabbed a bottle of water, and proceeded to the conference room, where I met for over an hour with a group of delightfully creative mothers. At the end of the day, when I finally collapsed in the comfort of my hotel bed, I whispered a quick "Thank you, Lord," and went unconscious until the next morning.

As I traveled home, tired but satisfied, I thought about the wonderful weekend and the enthusiastic mothers I was able to connect with. I also thought about my "almost migraine" and how the aura miraculously disappeared. I knew that God, in his grace and mercy, had given me the strength I needed for that day.

A few days later, as I was walking down the church hallway on my way to our Bible study room, a friend stopped to say hello. After we hugged and exchanged greetings, she added, "Oh, guess what? On Saturday morning I was cleaning my son's room and I found your book *Cracks in the Sidewalk* under his bed. So I stopped and prayed and said, 'God, wherever she is, just bless her and use her, and give her the strength she needs for today.'"

As tears welled in my eyes, I told her my "almost migraine" story, and we both marveled at how God had used her prayer in such a powerful way.

When the Holy Spirit nudges us to pray for someone, we must respond. I believe that God uses the prayers of our friends and family to intercede for us. It is also important to let others know that you pray for them. If my friend hadn't told me that she had prayed for me that day, neither of us would have been aware of the answer to her prayer.

And if you ever find a copy of *Cracks in the Sidewalk* under someone's bed, you will know what to do!

A Friend
Who Will Pray

It's nice to have a friend
  to call on the phone,
Or a friend you can visit
  when you are all alone.

It's nice to have a friend
  who has thoughtful words to say,
But the best kind of friend
  is a friend who will pray.

It's nice to have a friend
  who tries to understand,
It's nice to have a friend
  when you need an extra hand.

A friend can offer comfort
  when things don't go your way,
But the best kind of friend
  is a friend who will pray.

It's nice to have a friend
  who is honest and kind,
For true and loyal friends
  are difficult to find.

Though friends may come and go,
  some will always stay,
And the best kind of friend
  is a friend who will pray.

Warmhearted People

All people smile in the same language.

Uncle Ben's Quote Book

It was not my idea of a summer vacation spot, but since we were traveling through Alaska we decided to visit the northernmost point in the United States; it was only a short plane ride away. As we departed the small plane and walked toward the terminal, the bitter wind whipped through my body. Did I mention it was July?

Point Barrow, Alaska, is a popular tourist attraction—not because there is anything to see or do but because the people who visit can say they've been there. Most people arrive in the morning and leave in the evening, but we decided to go for the whole effect and spend the night.

We were greeted at the airport by our tour guide, who escorted us to our twenty-four-hour transportation service—a rickety old school bus with broken windows. On the seats were hooded, fur-lined coats for those who were not prepared for the chilly temperatures.

Our first stop was at a wide-open area where we could walk around on the tundra. I remembered learning about tundra in sixth-grade geography, yet never having a clue as to what it actually was. *So this is the tundra,* I thought to myself as I gingerly stepped on dormant vegetation, making footprints in the semi-frozen, spongy soil.

Our next stop was the ocean, where we posed for pictures in front of gigantic whale bones dramatically arranged on the beach to capture the attention of the tourists. The gray, misty sky hovered over the ocean, erasing any trace of the horizon. Everything was gloomy and depressing, and I wanted to go home.

My disposition improved as we dined at a Mexican restaurant called North of the Border. The hostess, Elly, worked the crowd like a pro, filling coffee cups and daring her customers to come out for the polar bear dip. Since I was freezing with all my clothes on, I decided to pass, but Bob and the kids accepted the challenge. At 10:00 that evening—since the sun doesn't set in July—we met Elly on the shore. One by one, Bob, Robby, Scott, and Teri became members of the Barrow Polar Bear Club by submerging themselves in the icy waters of the Arctic Ocean. It was the first time I had laughed since our arrival.

It was weird going to bed in broad daylight, but we finally went to sleep at 1:00 A.M. The next morning, we walked to a bakery where we purchased some bagels and honey butter for breakfast. We then met up with our tour guide and boarded the bus for more scheduled events.

We stopped at the high school, where local Native Americans educated and entertained us. Dressed in colorful costumes and furry boots, the children performed native dances while the men beat steady rhythms on sealskin drums. In daily life these same children run around in Levi's jeans and Nike tennis shoes, but in an effort to preserve their culture, they learn traditional customs through the education system.

After several dance exhibitions, the people began singing songs in their native tongue. As I watched them perform and studied their faces, I was touched by their kind looks and their warmth. Dark-haired children with piercing eyes sang from their souls and melted my heart. Suddenly, I wasn't cold anymore. When they closed their program with an English song I had learned in Sunday school, I had all I could do to keep the tears from spilling down my cheeks:

> God will take care of you, through every day, o'er all the way.
> He will take care of you, God will take care of you.

There is a chance I may never return to Point Barrow, Alaska, but now I can say that I've been there. It is a cold, dreary land, but it is filled with beautiful people whose kindness and warmth could melt an iceberg.

A Lesson from the Elephants

A friend loves at all times.

Proverbs 17:17a

I was hardly expecting to experience an emotional moment while sitting in a theater in Phoenix, Arizona—but that's where it happened!

Eager to trade our northern December temperatures for a milder climate, fourteen-year-old Teri and I had joined Bob on a weekend business trip to Phoenix. On Friday evening, we found ourselves driving through town, hoping for something interesting to appease our desire for entertainment. The local museum advertised the showing of *Elephants in Africa* in their recently completed IMAX theater. We parked our car, purchased tickets, and found seats in the center of the modern theater. Surrounded by hi-tech audio equipment and an enormous screen, we were prepared to *experience* the film.

The *National Geographic*-type movie documented the day-by-day experiences of a clan of African elephants. The group is called a clan because they are biologically related to one another. Brothers, sisters, aunts, uncles, parents, and grandparents travel the dry, dusty plains with the senior female elephant providing matriarchal leadership. The clan is continually on the move, in search of daily supplies of food and water. An elephant is able to walk when it is born, so it begins its journey with the clan when it is only a few hours old.

The film showed a baby elephant being born and following the clan on his wobbly legs. The baby gradually gained strength and was soon playfully interacting with the members of his clan. If there is an ample supply of food and water, the baby elephant continues to thrive and matures into a strong, healthy adult elephant. If, however, food and water are scarce, the young elephant gradually weakens and eventually dies.

The young elephant depicted in this film was not able to obtain proper nourishment. Though he appeared to be doing well for a while, he soon became too weak to travel and finally died. The mother elephant hovered over her baby in denial, prodding his lifeless body with her powerful trunk in an attempt to get him back on his feet. When her repeated efforts failed, she understood the fate of her precious offspring and went into a period of mourning, refusing to travel for several days in order to stay by his side.

It was what I witnessed next that had me reaching into my pocket for my travel-size package of tissues. The film showed all the female elephants from the clan surrounding the mother elephant to comfort her until her time of grieving was over. They didn't encourage her to travel, and they didn't abandon her. They simply gave her emotional support with their physical presence. *What a beautiful picture of friendship!* I thought as I sopped up my tears and blew my dripping nose.

It is often difficult to know how to respond appropriately to a friend or loved one who is hurting. That evening I learned an important lesson from the elephants: Don't abandon your friends when they are grieving, and don't tell them to get on with their lives. Just be there.

Sisters

A sister is someone who cares about you,
And she knows you inside out.
She listens when you need to talk
No matter what it's about.

A sister can tell you your hair's too long,
Or it's time to cover the gray.
A sister can give you a certain look
And you know what she's trying to say.

A sister will laugh when you tell her a joke,
Even though the joke isn't funny.
A sister will tire of shopping
When she knows you've spent enough money.

A sister can always help you decide
If the earrings you're wearing are right.
She'll let you borrow her favorite dress
When you're going out for the night.

A sister will not order cheesecake
When she knows you are on a diet.
And even though she loves tofu,
She'll never make you try it.

A sister will tell you your kids are great,
Even though she knows their faults.
She'll give you her secret recipe
For frosty chocolate malts.

She's someone with whom you can laugh or cry,
She's someone with whom you can pray.
She's someone that you can call on the phone
Any time of the night or day.

There are many kinds of sisters,
Though it's hard to tell them apart.
Sisters by birth, sisters in Christ,
Or sisters heart-to-heart.

Merry Christmas

For to us a child is born, to us a son is given, and the government will be on his shoulders. And he will be called Wonderful Counselor, Mighty God, Everlasting Father, Prince of Peace.

Isaiah 9:6

Christmas is the most popular holiday in America. But even though it occurs only one day each year, in the month of December, we are reminded of it throughout every season of the year. Christmas items linger on clearance tables until they are replaced by Valentine's Day leftovers. They show up again in mid-July, when eager shoppers search for bargains at crowded sidewalk sales. The first chilly autumn evening suggests that Christmas is around the corner. And by October, in most shopping malls, the pumpkins and cornstalks are barely noticeable among the wreaths, reindeer, and decorated evergreens.

People have been celebrating this holiday for centuries. But throughout the years, commercialism, the pressure of social events, and greed have robbed many of the true joy of this blessed holiday.

One year, as I was taking boxes out of our Christmas closet and unpacking the items, I was delighted to discover a beautiful, hand-painted nativity set that we had purchased the prior year.

For some reason, I had completely forgotten about it, and finding it was as much fun as opening a present. As I unwrapped the individual pieces and put them on a table in our foyer, I thought about the fact that many people celebrate Christmas every year but completely forget the true meaning.

Christmas is the celebration of God's Son sent to earth in human form. He healed the sick, taught the truth, and calmed the storms. He is King of kings and Lord of lords. Through his death and resurrection, God offers eternal life to all who believe in him. That's what Christmas is all about—but somehow the world has forgotten.

The Christmas Closet

I dug inside the closet
To find our Christmas things.
I found some scented candles
And a silver bell that rings.

I dusted off the reindeer
And set them on a shelf.
I found some handmade ornaments
I made all by myself.

I took the children's stockings
And hung them in a row,
Beneath a pinecone wreath
With a crimson velvet bow.

The quaint ceramic village
I handled with great care.
I placed it on the mantel
With wisps of angel hair.

I found some lights and garlands
And strung them on the tree,
Then put an angel on the top
For everyone to see.

And then I found the manger scene
So neatly tucked away.
I gently picked up every piece
And put it on display.

Joseph and the wise men,
A shepherd with his sheep,
And virgin Mary watching
As the Christ child lay asleep.

Somehow I was reminded
By this sweet Nativity,
That God took on the form of man
In all humility.

He came to earth to live and die
Because of his great love,
That we might have eternal life
And reign with him above.

So as you celebrate this time
With gifts and garlands too,
Remember, please, to honor him,
The one who died for you.

December Woman

She is busy every day,
From morning until night,
With toys to buy and gifts to wrap,
And Christmas cards to write.
She needs to sew a costume
For her daughter's fourth-grade play,
And wash the sheets and towels
For the guests who've come to stay.

She needs to bake some cookies
And decorate her home,
And bring a few poinsettias
To her friends who live alone.
She needs to plan a dinner
With fancy gourmet food,
While everyone expects her
To maintain a cheerful mood.

Though all these things are wonderful
And surely must be done,
She finds that she grows weary
And is always on the run.
She has no time to pause
In the middle of the day
To steal some quiet moments,
To read God's Word or pray.

But somehow she's reminded
At this busy time of year,
That Jesus is the reason
For all this Christmas cheer.
For God sent his beloved Son
From heaven down to earth.
And Christmas is the time for us
To celebrate his birth.

He came to offer peace and hope,
To heal our pain and strife.
To those who put their trust in him,
He gives eternal life.
And so she gets down on her knees
And bows her head in shame.
She thanks the Lord for his great love,
And for the One who came.

Then she adds this little prayer,
"Oh, Lord, please let it be,
That all my friends and family
Would see Jesus Christ in me."

Gifts

Some give gifts of gold and silver,
Some give clothes to wear.
Others shop for porcelain dolls
Or talking teddy bears.

Candy canes and choo-choo trains
Make young children smile,
But gifts wrapped up in boxes
Only last a little while.

Hugs and kisses don't wear out,
Kindness never fades,
Words of praise and compliments
Come in many shades.

Laughter needs no batteries,
It works in any weather,
And nothing is more comfortable
Than spending time together.

When searching for that perfect gift
Becomes a great concern,
Why not give the gift of love?
It often gets returned.

Thank You, God, for Children

Thank you, God, for children,
For laughter in the halls.
For rosy cheeks and hide-and-seek,
And smudges on the walls.

Thank you, God, for children,
For messy rooms to clean.
For wooden blocks and missing socks,
And faded, patched-up jeans.

Thank you, God, for children,
For questions that never end.
For A-B-C's and 1-2-3's,
And playing "let's pretend."

Thank you, God, for children,
For muddy hands and feet.
For soapy suds and slippery tubs,
And skin that's soft and sweet.

Thank you, God, for children,
For hugs and kisses too.
For bedtime tales of toads and snails
And saying, "I love you!"

Mothers

Mothers are made of smiles and tears
And hands that love to touch.
Mothers speak words of wisdom and truth
That little ones need so much.

Mothers have arms that comfort and hold;
Their kisses are soft and sweet.
Mothers are there to listen and care
And make every home complete.

Mothers are busy both day and night
Doing their motherly deeds.
It seems that mothers always know
Exactly what everyone needs.

Mothers are known for loving and giving,
And sharing their lives with others.
Their hearts are patient, tender, and kind.
Thank you, God, for mothers.

Crystal Bowman is a homemaker, speaker, poet, and lyricist. A former preschool teacher and the mother of three grown children, Crystal has written many children's books including several books in the Mothers of Preschoolers series. She is active in women's ministries and has written Bible study materials for women and children. Some of her books include *Cracks in the Sidewalk, If Peas Could Taste Like Candy, My ABC Bible—My ABC Prayers,* and *Mealtime Moments.* Crystal and her husband live in Grand Rapids, Michigan.

Journaling Pages